Trial by Fire

Tales from the dawn
of the computer age

Stephen M. Buck

outskirtspress
DENVER, COLORADO

Trial by Fire
Tales from the dawn of the computer age
All Rights Reserved.
Copyright © 2012 Stephen M. Buck
v4.0

Cover Image provided by Goodwin Steel Castings

Outskirts Press, Inc.
http://www.outskirtspress.com

ISBN: 978-1-4327-9472-9

Library of Congress Control Number: 2012911203

Outskirts Press and the "OP" logo are trademarks belonging to Outskirts Press, Inc.

PRINTED IN THE UNITED STATES OF AMERICA

Dedicated to my wife Sheila, the love of my life, who has supported me through the good times and the bad times for the past fifty years.

Contents

Foreword

It all began several years ago in a conversation that I had with my son's father-in-law, Ed. Ed's specialty was video, and he had done an amazing job documenting his own life. Every time I met him over at my son's house he would insist that I write my story. I was shocked....I couldn't imagine that anyone would be interested. But Ed would not leave it alone, so I began, slowly to work some ideas around in my head. I discarded most of them out of hand....And then I began to notice something....Even though I had been retired for years, I would dream every night that I was back in a power plant or factory, trying to solve computer problems or write programs. This was bizarre...I asked other people if they had the same experience and they just looked at me blankly. Obviously, there was something inside me that needed to come out...It took me two years to begin the process.

Once I began to write, however, it was like opening a crack in the dam... The words just wouldn't stop coming out...Within weeks I had documented all of my experiences working for Honeywell International. As I wrote, I began to see a common theme emerging, so I sought to organize the writings in a way that would make sense to the general reader. As I read and re-read my chapters, it slowly came to my realization that I was documenting a period in time that existed for only a few years;

much like the Old West....But there was a deeper meaning also...People around me, and especially young people like my grandsons, had absolutely no idea "what Grandpa did". I tried explaining it to them, but there was nothing about it to which they could relate. And that made me more and more convinced that I had to create something to pass down to future generations. No one else, to my knowledge, had ever written about the early days of computing and the bizarre cultural and political problems that we faced as we sought to export our technology to third world countries.

Today, computer technology has brought the world together, uniting countries and cultures with a common experience. But that was not the case in the 'seventies. Every computer was different and every culture was unique...There was no Internet and no easy way for one computer to communicate with another. And there were no personal computers or even microprocessors. Computers filled whole rooms and were extremely costly, no to mention the fact that they were "user vicious". No two computers were programmed the same way...Essentially, there were no "common threads" between machines and every system had to have its own highly-trained hardware and software engineer to support it...Failures were common, and each country sought to deal with the challenge of computing in its own individual way. Some saw the computer as a status symbol to impress its customers, regardless of whether it worked or not. Others, in nuclear power plants trusted the computer to control certain processes but refused to let it actually move the control rods that regulated the reactor output. And still other customers used it for data acquisition or "information only", refusing to let the computer take any action in the real world that might potentially cause harm. In those early days, the fear of computers in industry was so great that Honeywell actually sold computer-driven panel-board gages with moving needles to make plant operators think they were controlling individual, analog instruments…

Those days are gone forever. Refineries and chemical plants now run totally on computer control. The whole world has adopted the PC and

Microsoft software. Computers have now become so user friendly and so reliable that even the most computer-illiterate person can sit down and communicate with the entire world. No longer are highly-trained hardware and software specialists necessary to support computer systems, which have become so cheap that, if they don't work, they can be replaced for a few hundred dollars.

The world has moved on from those early days and it's probably all for the best. Today no one really wants to know or cares how a computer thinks. Microprocessors have made all of that knowledge obsolete... Looking back, I am appalled at how much of the training I endured is now irrelevant. The original GE 4020 computer system used a ten megahertz processor that lasted from its inception in 1963 until 1979 when the Honeywell 4500 was introduced. Today, processors are outdated in a year or less...

In the last few years of my career, with the addition of the PC to our systems, technology accelerated at an even faster pace. I spent many hours in classes taking courses in the Windows NT operating system. When I finished, I was told that Windows NT was obsolete, so I moved on, taking half a dozen courses in Windows 2000, which, by the time I finished, was also obsolete. I began to realize that I was on the Bill Gates Treadmill. Here I was, a 60-year-old man, taking community college courses with kids who were one-fourth my age. "What's wrong with this picture?" I thought to myself. This was insane...I was spending more time taking computer courses at Honeywell in Phoenix and community college than I was actually working on computer systems. The handwriting was on the wall...As technology increased and the economy worsened, more and more customers began to cancel Honeywell contracts and support their own systems. I had jumped from location to location to stay ahead of the curve but our local office was now down to three people, including me, which I interpreted as a sign of impending doom... Finally, at age 64, I turned in my gear and retired.

Prologue

It was 1962 and I had just been discharged from the Marine Corps. I was living with my wife Sheila at my in-laws while I looked for a job in the New Brunswick, New Jersey area. My in-laws, Martin and Gertrude were the best people in the world and I considered myself very lucky. Martin was a national level executive in the Boy Scouts of America and his wife, Gertrude was his main supporter.

I looked through the want ads in the New Brunswick paper… Nothing…Sheila, my wife of fifty years, and I met at Pennsylvania State University. I was a junior with two years of aeronautical engineering behind me and she was a freshman. It was love at first sight and we plunged into marriage fourteen months later. But now it was time to get a job to support the family.

I looked and looked. One day I came across an ad for a technician at Johnson and Johnson Research in North Brunswick. I applied immediately and was hired. The job involved the testing of pharmaceutical products. It was fairly routine, mostly consisting of making viscosity measurements on baby lotion using a Brookfield Viscometer and recording the results. I yearned for something more interesting. It was then I discovered the Analytical Lab, where assays were done to determine the concentration of active ingredients in samples of experimental products. There was an opening, so I applied and was accepted.

The job required that I go to college at night and major in chemistry, so I submitted my application to Rutgers University. I was accepted rapidly, which pleased me. However, I was not prepared for the treatment that I was about to receive... Rutgers "trashed" most of my Penn State credits and insisted that I repeat many courses that I had taken previously. But the greatest insult of all was the requirement that I take TWO YEARS of English Composition. Penn State had exempted me from taking ANY English Composition because I had gotten high marks in the essay part of my entrance exam. This was an affront almost too grievous to bear. Rutgers fancied itself to be part of the "Ivy League" in those days and insisted upon forcing English composition down students' throats, whether they needed it or not. And, to add insult to injury, at graduation, chemistry degree candidates were awarded a Bachelor of Arts degree, while business students were awarded a Bachelor of Science... This was the worst kind of disturbed academic thinking... Everything the university taught was somehow a "science": everything, that is, except physics and chemistry. It reminded me of some sort of medieval mind set... Maybe it was Alchemy they were actually teaching...

But I bit the bullet and plunged ahead with my second academic career. Working and going to school at night, I was to discover, was a tough grind. I completed a year of General Chemistry, which I had already passed at Penn State, and then proceeded on to a second year of Analytical Chemistry, which I truly loved. My career as an Analytical Technician at J&J prepared me well for the course and I excelled. The next year was Organic Chemistry, which I began to dislike with a passion. Unlike Analytical Chemistry, Organic Chemistry was mostly about memorizing organic molecular structures and organic reactions, which I hated. There was absolutely nothing mathematical about it, as there had been with Analytical Chemistry. I made little models of organic molecules with toothpicks and Styrofoam balls and hung them from the ceiling. Interesting this was not...

But as bad as the Organic Chem lectures were, the labs were even worse. All labs were held from six to eleven p.m., which, after a day of work, was a killer. I had missed one lab because of illness, so one night I was working on a makeup. Unfortunately, I had missed the instructions, so I followed the manual, running through a chain of organic reactions that were designed to produce the desired end product. Halfway through the reaction chain the whole experiment blew up…Huge clouds of white smoke filled the lab…people were hanging out the open windows, choking and coughing…The smoke was Magnesium Oxide, produced by the same sort of reaction that destroyers in World War II used to create a smokescreen….My lab instructor appeared out of the fog…He was very upset…I told him that I had just followed the directions in the manual. He looked mad…"You should have just followed the instructions we gave last week and added only one-tenth of those reagents!" he shouted. Of course, he could have told me that to begin with…

It got worse. This time I was more determined than ever to produce the proper organic end product, so I carefully followed every direction. We always began with a starting material and then proceeded through a chain of reactions until the final product was produced. It is the nature of all organic solid compounds, because of their unique structure, to have different melting points, so the final test was to take a small sample in a tiny glass tube and slowly raise the temperature until it melted. Any contaminants, caused by sloppy procedures, would lower the melting point, so this was the final test of purity…

No matter how rapidly I worked, it always took me until 10:30 or so to finish up. I absolutely could not understand how other students could be walking out the door at 9:00 p.m. It was extremely irritating, but I kept working away…I finished and checked my melting point… ARRRGGGHHH…It wasn't even close…In desperation, I tried repeating the last several reactions, but the results were the same…It was getting late…My lab instructor came over. "What is your melting point?" he asked me….I was embarrassed…I told him and tried to explain…"Never mind", he said. "But it's…" Before I could protest, he said "It's good" and walked away…I couldn't believe it. I handed in the sample and walked out the door. How could it be good?

And then I found out…One of the lab instructors had become suspicious of the samples that were being handed in. Some were "too good" to be produced with the simple lab equipment that we had available. He suspected that the students, working for the pharmaceutical industries in the area, were just obtaining the purified end products from work, "dry labbing" it, handing in the samples, and departing early. So he devised a plan.

Instead of giving us the regular starting material, he gave us slightly different starting materials with an organic structure that had a subtle variant. Using it, we would end up with a different end product and a different melting point. Anyone whose sample melted in agreement with the manual would be severely disciplined. The cheaters were identified and punishments were handed out. No one was expelled, but several were set back severely in their careers.

Time went by…I finished my organic chemistry course and returned again to Rutgers for a semester of physical chemistry. I still enjoyed doing analytical procedures at work, but school was getting increasingly boring. Unfortunately, spending my life in a laboratory was making me feel more and more like an inmate. There were huge plate glass windows at the end of the benches that looked out on the "real world". I would stare out of them every day, like a prisoner looking out from his cell…Yard time was 12:00 to 1:00 and then back to the cell…I found diversion by purchasing a small boat and teaching myself how to sail… In the winter I built a telescope and took up astronomy…And then I set up a darkroom to develop the photographs I took through my telescope…It was still not enough, so I took a course in Ham Radio… Anything to reach out and touch the world around me…

At home, things were beginning to change. It was now 1966 and we had two children, David and James, and daughter Susan on the way.

Supporting the family on a research technician's salary was extremely difficult, and was soon going to be worse. And then it happened…I got promoted….Now I had to work in a windowless room assisting a research chemist in the development of new analytical techniques…It was a disaster…Whenever he left for vacation, I had absolutely nothing to do for weeks on end. At least, in the old days, I could work independently doing analytical procedures on the routine batches of samples brought over from the main building. But this was ridiculous…I could put up with anything but pretending to be busy. It was particularly difficult when I was forced to be idle at work when I had car repairs or other urgent issues at home that needed my attention…Al, my boss, was unable to understand why I hated this dependent type of position, so he used it as a pretext to sign me up for "aptitude tests" to determine what my "real interests" were…The test results indicated that I had aptitudes in engineering, chemistry and physics…Not too much help there…I think Al secretly wanted to get rid of me…I was a little too outspoken, independent, and non-deferential…I could not accept my role in the rigid academic hierarchy that pervaded the research community…This was a problem that I was going have with corporate management for the rest of my life…

And so it was on that one particular evening in the summer while I was working under my '57 Ford, replacing the universal joint on the drive shaft that my friend, Frank showed up. Frank and I met at the Philadelphia Navy Yard when we were in the service and were good friends, traveling home together on weekends on the Jersey Central Railroad. We would see just how many beers we could finish off between Philadelphia and Westfield, New Jersey, where I got off…I remember setting the record of six Pabst Blue Ribbons over the hour and a half journey.

Frank sat on the bumper of the car and talked to me while I tried to fit the universal joint onto the drive shaft. He was working as a field service representative for Honeywell in Union, New Jersey. I knew that he had a company car and visited factories, where he did troubleshooting and repair on control devices for industrial processes. It intrigued the hell out of me…The more he told me about his work, the more interested I became. "You know," he said, "You should apply for a job".

That hit me like a ton of bricks. He explained that the starting salary was $500 a month, more than the $110 a week I was earning after almost 5 years at J&J. "Wow", I thought, "$500 a month and a company car!". It was almost too good to be true…My '57 Ford was wearing out…I could envision driving around in a brand new company car…

But I did not have the experience that Frank had. He was a machinist's mate in the Navy and was very experienced with boilers and other control systems that were unfamiliar to me. We had to develop a plan. Frank told me about the testing that he had gone through and we discussed it in detail. First there was an intelligence test, followed by a scientific and engineering knowledge and aptitude test. Lastly, there was an electronics and electrical test. I felt very confident in everything but the electronics test, and especially the part where it required drawing the schematic diagram of a transistor amplifier. Frank lent me electronic books and I studied transistors, which were a totally alien species to me. I knew that if I could get past the front door and into the twelve week Honeywell training course at Fort Washington, Pennsylvania, I could learn everything I needed to know. I was very impressed with the company and its training policies…

I couldn't wait to apply… I discussed my plans with Joanie, an analytical lab technician that I worked with at J&J . "Honeywell?" she said, "I know the personnel director"…"Really?", I replied…Joanie knew him from her Catholic Youth Fellowship group and they were good friends. I tucked the information away for future use…

Finally, I worked up the courage to call the personnel director at Honeywell and make an appointment. I walked into his office at 11:00 a.m. and introduced myself. He looked bored. He examined my application. I explained my background, but he was unimpressed. "You have no process control background", he stated. I protested that I had an engineering background and worked as a technician in an analytical lab. "But you have no field experience", he protested. "These service reps have to walk into factories where the equipment is down and bring the systems back to life", he said. I told him that, with the training that Honeywell supplied, I would be able to do that. He remained unconvinced.

I was out of ammunition…but not quite…I had one bullet left. Then I told him about Joanie at J&J, and suddenly his attitude changed. "OK", he said, "Come back at 1:00 and take the tests"…WOW ! I couldn't believe it…I had actually pulled it off…But what was I going to do for the next several hours? I drove over to Echo Lake, a small lake where I had rented rowboats as a kid… I absolutely couldn't stand it… The intensity was so overwhelming I couldn't sit still. I never wanted any job so much in my life…If I couldn't get it I would be devastated.

I sat on a park bench and watched the ducks. It was just too much… I had to get up and burn off the energy that was building up…I walked furiously up and down the asphalt paths by the lake for over an hour…Finally, it was time to return. I entered the Honeywell office and was directed into a small room for testing. I was handed the first test, the Rutherford Adult Intelligence Test. Unbelievable! What a break! Unbeknownst to my testers I had spent an entire semester in Psychology 101 at Rutgers studying this very test. I knew every answer cold…I knew I could easily hit the maximum I.Q. score of 135. My confidence began to build. Then came the engineering and scientific test. With all the physics and chemistry courses I had taken, this was not a problem. And then there was the electrical and electronics knowledge test. I did well on the electrical part, thanks to my physics courses, but the electronic part was new to me. I drew the schematic drawing of the transistor amplifier from memory, not really understanding what I was doing…

I went home that night feeling I had done well…The next morning, at J&J, I got a call from the Honeywell service manager. "How soon can you start?" he asked. I was shocked. I told him "two weeks"…He was disappointed because I couldn't start right away…

And that was the beginning of my career with Honeywell, a love affair that would last over 37 years. Through good times and bad, I loved my job. Eventually, computer technology would become so ubiquitous, so cheap, so dependable and so user friendly that selling computer support contracts at Honeywell rates would be next to impossible. The era of highly trained field engineers was rapidly drawing to a close and I was very proud to have been a part of it. The downturn in the economy and the acquisition of our company by Allied Signal would finally finish off what had been an outstanding career with an outstanding company.

The Beginning of the Beginning

And now I am retired, but not really….Every night I am back on the job, in the factories, trying to understand problems with computer and control systems…racking my brains in my dream state…not able to write the exact program or puzzle out the exact fix… When will it ever end? Is it possible to be so in love with your job that, if you do not perform it in the daytime then you will do it at night in your dreams? Thirty seven years of working in the field for Honeywell solving computer and control problems had taken its toll.

I do not know the answer…The world has changed a lot since the early days of instrumentation and process control, a world that I entered in 1966. Those were the days before transistors, before integrated circuits and, yes, way before microprocessors and computers. Engineers in those days had to devise ways to measure variables such as steam flow, temperature and pressure without the aid of electronic devices.

Each application was ingenious yet simple. Steam flow was always an important measured variable, especially in power plants. But how to measure something so difficult, especially considering the several hundred pounds of pressure in the mains? The answer was to put a restrictor, called an orifice plate, in the steam mains. The pressure drop across the orifice was proportional to the square root of the steam flow, as it turned out, so to measure it, a U-tube device was constructed with one leg of the U-tube connected upstream and one tube connected downstream of the orifice plate. The U-tube was filled with mercury, allowing each side to seek a level in accordance with the pressure sensed from the orifice plate. The differential level between the two legs, then, became proportional to the square root of the actual steam flow.

But how to indicate this measurement? The answer was simple: Because mercury is 13.6 times the density of water, it became an easy matter to float a steel weight on top of the mercury in the tube and to connect a rod which moved up and down with the flow. The rod was then directly attached to a linkage in the recorder housing which drove a pen upon a chart. The chart was printed in a square root format which accurately reflected the steam flow, and a mechanical "totalizer" was linked to the pen which showed total volume of steam consumed in a given period of time.

And on it went...One of the best ways to measure temperature was by use of a thermocouple, of which there were many classes, some of the most common being class J, K, and T. The principal was simple: The measured emf (electromotive force) was proportional to the difference in temperature between the measured end and the reference end. But how could two wires generate a millivoltage? It all depended upon the type of metal used. In type J thermocouples, for instance, the metals were iron and constantan; in type T couples the metals were copper and constantan and in type K couples, the metals were chromel and alumel. Each generated a specific millivoltage over a specific range of temperatures. For low temperatures, a type T was often used; for higher temperatures a type J, and for higher temperatures still a type K was used.

But, before the age of solid state devices, how could these tiny (thousandth of a volt) measurements be made? The answer was always the same: The Wheatstone Bridge, which was known as a "null balance potentiometer". The principle was simple...a "standard cell" generated a precise voltage, which was compared against the incoming thermocouple voltage. The two voltages were "bucked" against each other using a calibrated potentiometer until a very sensitive current measuring device, called a "light beam galvanometer" indicated that the voltages were "nulled out", meaning that no current was flowing between them because they were exactly equal. The potentiometer voltage was then read, following which the "reference" junction temperature was measured using a mercury-in-glass thermometer at the terminals where the thermocouple was connected. After the reference junction was converted to millivolts by means of a table for the specific type of thermocouple, the following equation was solved by hand for the measured junction voltage.

EMF=Measured Junction – Reference Junction

Once this was done, using the same handbook, the measured junction millivoltage was then converted to degrees. To perform these measurements we carried around a 10 pound box called a "Honeywell 2720 Potentiometer" which was powered by a huge 1.5 volt battery and which contained a standard cell. We could either measure the degrees from the actual thermocouple or, after calculation, generate the exact millivoltage and apply it to the temperature measuring device in question to determine the accuracy of its calibration.

But all of this led to much mischief…I can recall my friend and mentor in those days, Frank, deciding to check out a thermocouple installed in the top of a refractory in a brick oven. Frank walked over the insulation on top of the refractory and proceeded to examine the head of the thermocouple when the plant manager came by and stopped dead in his tracks. "Tell him to get off there, right now!", he said, "Those bricks in the top of the refractory are only held together by gravity!" Luckily, Frank managed to work his way slowly off the top of the refractory without collapsing the whole thing and falling into the several-thousand degree furnace.

Looking back, it's amazing that any of us survived those days. I can recall visiting one of our customers, Evans Products, in Aberdeen, Washington. I had designed a special instrument panel which included a temperature controller and a secondary meter to indicate the position of the gas valve motor, which corresponded to the amount of heat being generated by the burner. I had installed the panel on one of the customer's plywood dryers and on this trip I was checking the installation to see if it was working properly. I noticed, unfortunately, that the gas valve position meter did not appear to be accurately tracking the position of the gas valve, so I decided to climb up on top of the dryer to clean the slidewire on the motor. The first thing I noticed, when I began the climb to the top of the dryer was that my eyes were stinging. As I approached the top of the dryer the stinging increased and I began to notice some difficulty breathing. By blinking my eyes rapidly I was able to see well enough to proceed to the motor. I took off the slidewire cover and began to clean the slidewire with a fine piece of emery paper. I finished the job and replaced the cover, coughing violently. Suddenly, I heard a siren…As I slowly made my way back to the ladder I saw a fire truck enter the side door. The truck came to a halt and firemen jumped off and began to hose down the burning dryer. Luckily, I made it back to the ladder and down to the ground before the whole thing burst into flames…

Those were the days…As I look on the internet to see if Evans Products still exists, I find that they declared bankruptcy in 1985, ten years after I left the world of instrumentation for the world of process computer systems. "Just as well," I thought to myself, remembering one of my last calls at the plant. For better or for worse, our local salesman, seeking to expand our contract at Evans Products, sold them a maintenance contract on their package boiler. This was somewhat terrifying to me, especially considering the fact that they always ran it "full bore" at 150 pounds steam pressure, which was the maximum that the boiler could handle, and the noise was deafening.

One of my tasks was to make sure the boiler flame safeguard programmer functioned properly, so when the mill was down for maintenance I would put it through its paces. The program started off with a "purge" of all gases in the firebox using a large forced draft fan. The fan brought outside air into the firebox and displaced any existing gases and ran for five minutes. Once complete, the programmer initiated a "trial for ignition" in which the pilot gas valve was opened and an ignition transformer energized. If the pilot successfully lit, as determined by a current coming back from the flame rod, the main gas valve would be energized, lighting off the main burner. If all went well, steam pressure would mount in the boiler until it reached the 150 p.s.i. setpoint, at which time the main burner would be cycled down to low fire. It was a beast... Every month I dreaded making the service call...

Then, one morning at 1:00 a.m. the phone rang...The call was from Evans Products...I could hardly believe the news...The boiler had exploded and driven the entire front end through the wall. Luckily, no one was hurt... I got on my clothes, packed my tools and headed out, arriving there about 3:00 a.m.... There was the boiler with the entire front end missing and it was up to me to figure out what happened... ARRGGGGHHH, I thought to myself...What in the world am I going to do?

I talked to the chief engineer and then to the electrician and maintenance people. Slowly, little by little, I began to get the whole picture. The nature of a burner flame is somewhat different than is generally understood. In any burner the mixture of gas and air has an outward velocity, a fact that is well established. What is not generally understood is that the flame also has a velocity which opposes the velocity of the fuel supply. What this means is that, as the fuel flows outward from the burner tip, the flame burns inward, towards the burner tip. When both the flame velocity and the fuel velocity are matched, the flame is stable and burns properly at the end of the burner. Unfortunately, the maintenance people at Evans had adopted a concept of combustion that did not match this reality.

And now, the problem: when the pilot burner became hard to light, the first thing the maintenance people did was to increase the gas pressure on the regulator, which increased the fuel velocity. When the fuel velocity became greater than the flame velocity, the flame began to move away from burner tip making it highly unstable and prone to extinction. And when the flame went out, it became increasingly difficult to light.

And that was precisely what had happened. When the package boiler pilot failed to light properly, maintenance people increased the fuel pressure by screwing down the regulator and increasing fuel velocity. When this failed to cause the pilot to light, the maintenance people removed the regulator altogether, causing the pilot gas pressure to go from several ounces to several pounds per square inch. When this failed to solve the problems, workers then replaced the "positive spring shut-off" pilot solenoid valve and gas line with a larger gas line and "gravity type" pilot gas valve which relied solely on gravitational force to close it. Unfortunately, the pilot gas valve was mounted at an angle of about 45 degrees, which made "gravity closure" somewhat questionable. However, the boiler was finally lit and production resumed.

The disaster scene was set. At approximately midnight on that fateful day, the gas company called to tell the plant to shut down their interruptible natural gas usage. Now there are two types of customers for natural gas. In winter, when supplies became limited, gas customers who purchased "interruptible" service at a lower rate were asked to curtail their usage in favor of "non-interruptible" customers who paid a premium. In this case, Evans paid the lower rate, so plans were laid to slowly shut off the natural gas supply valve while at the same time opening the valve from the propane tank in order to maintain fuel supply to the boiler.

Unfortunately, the shutdown of the natural gas valve and the opening of the propane valve were not synchronized properly, so the natural gas was shut off before the propane valve could be opened. Immediately the boiler flame was lost. Seconds later, the propane valve was opened, but there was no fire in the boiler. However, the replaced pilot valve with "gravity closure" had failed to close so propane gas at several p.s.i. now began to fill the hot firebox. As the firebox filled with propane, the operators discussed their options, unaware of the situation. Finally, one of the operators went to the boiler programmer and initiated a start. By this time, the hot firebox was totally filled with propane, so when the operator pushed the "start" button the first action the device did was to inject the final element needed for combustion....air. When the air purge hit the firebox there was instantaneous combustion. The entire front end of the boiler blew off and through the opposite wall. When the chief engineer came over to talk to me I had the gas turned on with my thumb over the pilot line. When I removed it, the raw gas blew through the pilot gas valve and into his face. I showed him the "gravity close" pilot gas valve stuck in the open position and he immediately understood what had happened.

But this was not the end of my experience with gas explosions. One of my other customers, Davis Wire, in Kent had managed to find an old gas heater from one of their sites, used as a "wire dryer'. The problem with the heater was that there was absolutely no "flame safeguard" installed. When I asked them how they lit the burner, they replied. "We just turn on the gas valve, toss a lit rag inside and hope for the best". Obviously that did not comply with modern safety requirements, so I re-built the heater controls with a Honeywell R4138A unit that programmed the combustion by sensing the burner flame with an ultra-violet detector known as a "purple peeper".

All went well with the installation and it worked properly except that sometimes the flame from the main burner would "bounce around" the firebox and momentarily out of view of the purple peeper, which would then falsely signal that the burner had lost its flame, causing a nuisance shutdown.

This was a tough one, I had to admit. The only solution that I could think of was to re-position the purple peeper so that the flame was always in its view. But to do that, I had to look into the firebox while it was operating to determine what the flame was doing. Unfortunately, the only way of observing the flame in operation was to remove the peeper and then "fool it" with a cigarette lighter while I looked into the burner port. At the time, I did not realize that the port that the peeper was looking into was actually the main gas line, so that when I removed the peeper and fooled it with a cigarette lighter, the entire space around my body began filling with natural gas. About thirty seconds later the gas cloud advanced to the cigarette lighter and I was engulfed in a ball of flame, scorching my eyebrows and my hair. "Thank God", I thought to myself, "I'm going to Phoenix for computer training. It's probably the only thing that's going to save me from blowing myself up." Weeks later, when I arrived at the Honeywell Process Control Division in Phoenix, I had my picture taken for an ID badge, scorched eyebrows, hair and all.

I thought I had escaped the curse of the "trial by fire", but I was mistaken…It was to follow me for the rest of my career. For the time being, however, I was experiencing a well-needed respite, traveling to Phoenix with my family in late December of 1974. Unlike the Seattle area, Phoenix was warm and sunny and no sooner had we reached our apartment than our three kids put on their bathing suits and headed for the pool. To their great surprise, there was no one there! Later, the apartment manager arrived in her parka to announce that no one goes swimming in Phoenix "until the temperature reaches 90 degrees".

And so it went. Ten of us, all experienced Honeywell field personnel from every part of the country, had been selected to be the first candidates for a nine month long training school at Process Control Division Phoenix, a computer division recently purchased from General Electric. In my case, however, it had not been a simple selection. I had come to the realization over the previous year that instrumentation systems were being replaced by process computer systems, so I had applied and been accepted by Honeywell Commercial Division in Seattle to train as a computer specialist on the Delta 2000 system. I had given my two week notice and was within two days of transferring to Commercial when a got a call from my branch manager, offering to send me to Phoenix if were to stay with the Industrial Division. I immediately accepted, declined the offer with the Commercial Division, and waited on pins and needles for six months for the training to begin.

At last our school commenced with a 12 week course on the mainframe, a 24-bit word length, 4020 Process Computer System, followed by a similar course on the mainframe 4010 Computer and the 4400 Computer System. Years later, I would also report to training on the 4500 and the 45000 system, the 316 and the TDC 2000 and TDC 3000 system. My head was spinning. There was virtually no free time for the whole duration of the training school. In non-class hours, we would go to the lab and write our machine language programs and test them out on the computers. A simple "name and address program" written in machine language with "automatic interrupts" enabled, required pages of binary code with appropriate timing and sequencing of data. We were all "burned out" by the end of the course. On the final weekend, we worked all day Saturday and Sunday to complete our assignments, filling the lab with heaps of soda cans, loaded ash trays and cast off computer print-outs. There was no "high level language" here...every bit of data had to be laboriously written in octal and ASCII code. Unfortunately, the cleaning service did not work on the weekends, so when paying customers arrived on Monday morning and found the lab to be a disaster area, we were severely chastised. Luckily, we had all finished with our programming assignments by that time.

The training school, in those days, was a really minimal operation. Separated from the main factory on Peoria and the offices on Desert Cove Road, its location on Indian School Road in Phoenix was in the midst of a shopping center. General Electric, in its final days before the Honeywell purchase, had cut the operating budget to the entire computer division until it was operating "on a shoestring". The training school had only one copy machine, which was a "thermograph", a copier that existed before the Xerox days, and which operated using a "thermal imaging" technique. The copy paper was thermally sensitive, as it turned out, so if you took a copy of your program out in the blazing Phoenix sun, the image totally disappeared! But that was not the worst part...The school had only two computers, a mainframe 4020 and a 4010. All maintenance classes were held at night, from 4:00 p.m. until midnight, so we had to have all computers re-assembled and working before we went home in order for the software classes to use them in the daytime. And this was not always so easy. The instructors would usually "torture" us by failing to remove the "bugs" in the machines until the last minute, causing us to spend hours bent over our oscilloscopes examining every signal and attempting to deduce the cause of the failure.

Those early machines were totally underpowered by modern standards. Today's PC's have a 64 bit word length and clock speeds in the Gigahertz range, specifications that were unheard of in the 'seventies, before the advent of large scale or even medium scale integrated circuits. Instead, the entire 4010 processor, known as the AU or "arithmetic unit" was composed of small scale DTL (diode-transistor logic), with only one or two logic gates per chip. Unlike the microprocessor-driven PC of today, the 4010 had a "bit slice processor". For a 24-bit word length machine like the 4020 or 4010, the entire AU was made up of 6 full length boards, with 4 bits of word length per board. Data shifted serially or in parallel through registers, of which there were four main ones; the I or Instruction Register, the B or execution register, the A or auxiliary register and the P or program counter register. We became intimately familiar with each one and its functionality.

One morning, Jim, our instructor made an announcement. He had discovered a PBS TV documentary at 6:00 a.m. on a new type of electronic device. He knew that all of us were working hard on our training assignments, but he was asking us to make one more sacrifice ..."I know this is early in the morning, but this is something you should see". Everyone groaned...Finally one person took the bait. "So what is it?", he asked...Jim replied, "It's called a microprocessor", he said "and it might be significant one day"…And so it was on that spring morning in 1975, that I witnessed the birth of the first 4-bit microprocessor, a tiny machine that would grow up to revolutionize the world. I drank a cup of coffee and stared at the screen…It didn't look like much…I was not impressed…How could that possibly compete with our huge computer systems?… I took a shower and went to school.

In Honeywell classes we continued learning our craft, and as the days passed and our competence grew, we began the next phase of our training: field assignments. I visited IRS sites in Covington, Kentucky, Chamblis, Georgia, and Fresno, California, where we upgraded computers from 16 K of core memory to the newer, 32 K of solid state memory. Core memory, which is the only memory we had available at the beginning of the computer era, consisted of individual magnetic cores, wound by hand. A "pulse" of current would magnetize them in one direction for a digital "one" and in the opposite direction for a digital "zero". Because of its hand-made nature, core memory was extremely costly, not to mention low in capacity, with the typical size of memories being in the 16k to 32k range. Today's cell phones, which can have 4 gigabytes of memory, or 250,000 times as much, can be held in the palm of the hand.

Slowly, our stress levels decreased as we became more experienced in dealing with the intricacies of Honeywell computer systems. My life had now taken a turn for the better, but I was to learn that fate had not totally forgotten me. I graduated after nine months of training and field experience and returned home to Seattle, where I took up computer contracts at Olympic Pipeline in Renton, Washington, Bonneville Power in Vancouver and Burlington Northern Railroad in Pasco… I happily rejoiced in the thought that all of my boiler explosion days were long behind me. Several years went by. One day I answered a page from Phoenix with a chilling request. The recovery boiler at Stone Container in Missoula, Montana had just exploded, killing one person and seriously wounding two others. It was a Honeywell computer site and Honeywell management wanted me to perform an audit on the system, examining all historical data, to find out if our equipment was to blame.

I was shocked. I had no idea what a "recovery boiler" was or how to determine the cause of the explosion. Nor was I convinced that the other recovery boilers would not suddenly explode while I was investigating the cause of the failure. I approached the plant with sense of dread. The boiler operators on the existing recovery boilers were in a state of tension, thinking they could be "blown away" at any minute. I was told not to speak to them, so I talked to the plant engineers, and maintenance people. Slowly I learned how dangerous a recovery boiler could be.

In mills like Stone Container, wood chips were "digested" in a sulfuric acid solution to form a pulp, after which the pulp was bleached with chlorine for white paper or left in the original coloration for cardboard. The problem then becomes; how do you deal with the leftover sulfuric acid contaminated with wood resin? The answer is simple….Since the wood resin is combustible while the sulfuric acid is not, it is a relatively straightforward to fuel a boiler with the acid/resin mix. Once the firebox in the boiler is heated to temperature with a natural gas burner, the acid/resin mix is introduced. The resin then burns away, heating the water tubes in the boiler while the acid is returned to its natural state, forming a deep pool of concentrated sulfuric at a temperature of 500 degrees or better in the bottom of the firebox. The recovery boiler, it seemed, was actually a very efficient device, providing steam for the plant and recovered sulfuric acid for the digesters.

So far, so good. But there was one fatal flaw in this design. All it took was a small leak in one of the water tubes, and as little as several quarts of water descending to the pool of heated sulfuric acid below to cause the greatest steam explosion ever seen. When water transitions from liquid to vapor its volume increases by 1200 times, creating enough pressure inside the firebox to destroy the boiler and, in this case, cause it to plunge two floors down into the basement, destroying everything and everybody in its way.

No wonder everyone was in such a state of dread; with several more recovery boilers still in operation, how was anyone to know that it could not happen again? The tension was palpable…But how to figure out what happened, and, more to the point, how to finish the job and get the hell out of there before anything else exploded?

We worked late into the night. The Honeywell system controlled the gas firing of the boiler, so it was important to look at historical data to determine if the explosion could have been caused by an accumulation of natural gas in the firebox, in which case Honeywell could have been implicated. I examined all of the data collected by our computer system. Unfortunately, the system had been programmed to only store the latest data, so "looking back" and taking "snapshots" was critical before the old data was overwritten…

Finally, the task was completed. Unfortunately, the system had only been programmed to store data every 60 seconds, so the period of the explosion could not be analyzed dynamically. However it was sufficient to note that at the time of the explosion, the firebox pressure increased exponentially, driving the transmitter off scale, while at the same time the boiler exhaust gas analyzer noted that there were no combustibles in the exhaust gas, which proved that it had not been a "fire side" explosion. Later than evening, when a recovery boiler expert arrived at the site, he confirmed that, for an explosion that devastating, it had to be a "water side" explosion, meaning that the water tubes had leaked into the bed of molten sulfuric acid. Luckily, Honeywell was "off the hook" and I took the opportunity to write a report and depart the scene. Somehow, no matter what I did with my career, I could never quite escape the "trial by fire".

Inowroclaw

I was always the nail that stuck up and got hammered. My computer contracts in the Northwest were running well and required little support so I was an easy target. This time, however, I really couldn't complain...It was January of 1980 when I received a call to travel to Phoenix to assist in the staging area, where computer systems were set up for software development before they were shipped to their final destinations. It was bitterly cold in Seattle...The prospect of going to Phoenix was a welcome relief. My wife was jealous...

But getting to Phoenix in those early days was not an easy task. Usually, it required taking a Western Airlines 707 flight from Seattle to Los Angeles International and then changing planes for a flight from L.A. to Phoenix Sky Harbor. I always loved flying into Phoenix in the winter. Camelback Mountain and South and North Mountain stood like huge monoliths in the clear desert air.. Visibility was more than 100 miles with humidity below one percent. Walking out onto the sidewalk I could feel the heat of the sun. The sky was cloudless. Winter was nowhere in sight. It was like heaven.

I rented a car and drove into the parking lot at the Peoria Avenue manufacturing site for Honeywell. It was a bizarre structure, long and low and had been added onto many times. Mel was of the original

General Electric Engineers who had been in the startup of the computer organization in Phoenix. He had explained that the building G.E. had selected was actually an old "lettuce shed". I could certainly see the resemblance. But it housed a lot of memories, first for the original engineers and then, later, for me.

The original GE engineers had their work cut out for them back in the nineteen sixties, creating a computer system with operating software that could actually control a chemical plant, refinery, or nuclear reactor. Mel was an endless source of stories about those early days, most of which I have since forgotten. But the one that stuck with me was so bizarre that I remembered it in great detail.

It is important to understand that every high tech company has an "in house genius" and G.E. had one, who had been dubbed the "Father of RTMOS". RTMOS stood for the "Real Time Multiprogramming Operating System". Larry was that person, overweight, with thick glasses and a full dark beard. His reputation was well deserved as he worked on his creation night and day.

There was just one problem. The RTMOS operating system was constantly in a state of change to meet increasing business demands. Each time something was added or deleted, it caused issues somewhere else. A programmer friend of mine, Jim, confided to me that the operating system was a "mass of patches". Jim had discovered a simple instruction in the code to "branch" the program to upper memory. At the upper memory location he discovered another instruction to "branch back". Jim was puzzled…this was a "do nothing" part of the code in the operating system so he decided to eliminate it. Wrong... As soon as he made the fatal change the operating system crashed. That simple "branch up and branch back" do-nothing loop had been inserted as a "timing delay" to allow something else to happen. Jim never touched the RTMOS code after that..

So, the operating system code in its early phases was somewhat fragile. But the worst part was that, during its development, strange, inexplicable things could happen. Larry worked on the RTMOS code endlessly, but he could not make one problem appear. This really irritated him. It was killing his reputation. When he was away from the computer, the problem would appear…When he responded, it disappeared. He devised clever "traps" in the code to "catch" the problem, but, somehow, the problem failed to take the bait. This was becoming a personal battle against the forces of darkness…

Mel paused in his story to let the details sink in. He continued. Larry had worked late into Friday night on the "bug" in the system with no results. He was desperate. He finally hatched a plan…

Saturday morning arrived. Mel had some project issues to resolve so he had come in early to try to finish up. The building was empty and quiet so he settled down to work. Suddenly he heard some noise in the hallway, so he looked up. There was figure that he could not recognize. It had a long wig, funny glasses and a rubber nose…Mel looked closer…It was Larry! "SHHHHH!", said Larry, "I don't want it to recognize me!". Mel was stunned. He followed Larry into the computer room. Larry sat down at the console. Suddenly the problem appeared. "I found it" screamed Larry…"It didn't recognize me!" And so the problem was finally put to rest…

And that was pretty much "par for the course" in those early days. To be involved with computers in the 'sixties and 'seventies meant working on problems until you could not think straight anymore, and then coming back and doing it all over again. It was man against machine, but the machine had the edge, so to overcome it required total and absolute commitment.

And it was with those thoughts running through my head that I entered the Peoria Avenue plant and headed for the Ballroom, a large space in the center of the factory where the computers were staged. I knew Bud, the manager and all of the staging technicians from previous visits, so it was like "old home week". In those early days of computing, the Peoria Avenue plant was almost like a "family environment". On

Fridays, once a month and for a $5 contribution, everyone would be invited out to North Mountain Park for a steak barbecue sponsored by the company. There was nothing better than sipping a beer and enjoying a steak in the warm, dry air of a late winter afternoon as the sun cast long shadows over the desert scenery. It was a wonderful world.

But it was at lunch one day in the cafeteria that an opportunity arose that would have a dramatic impact upon my existence. One of the project managers that I knew came over and sat down at my table. "Would you be interested in installing a computer system in Poland?" he asked me. "Of course" I answered immediately. And then I thought about it for a second. "Wait a minute", I said, "Isn't Poland behind the Iron Curtain?" Of course it was. What was I thinking? Poland, since World War II had been part of the U.S.S.R. It was referred to as a Satellite Country in that it had a "puppet government" but was actually controlled by the Soviet Politburo in Moscow. We were in a Cold War with the USSR. Why in the world were we selling them a computer system?

It was a long story, and not a simple one. We were prevented from selling computer equipment or anything else to Soviet Russia. However, it was permitted by the U.S. government to sell computer systems or other computerized products to satellite countries provided that the technology was not the very latest. That was not a serious problem for Honeywell, since we were still using General Electric technology in our computer systems that dated back to the 'sixties. So, technically, it was a "go".

With these facts in mind, then, Honeywell applied for an export license to sell a 4400 computer system to Zaklady Chemiczne, a chemical company in Inowroclaw, Poland. This raised all kinds of eyebrows at the federal level and generated tons of paperwork, but finally, after 18 months of wrangling, the official export license had been issued. And now I was being asked to accompany a software engineer to install the system. Of course, I said "yes".

But dealing with the bureaucracy of a Communist nation was extremely difficult if not impossible. I kept in touch with Phoenix as the months rolled by and we attempted to establish the necessary credentials, work permits, and visas. Finally, the paperwork was done and the date of departure was scheduled in early May. But I still had not received my airplane tickets from the Polish Government. I complained to Phoenix, and then I got a strange call from Warsaw. It was the worst connection in the world and I struggled to make it clear that I needed a ticket to Poland from Seattle, Washington. I did not know if I had communicated successfully...

Weeks went by. The departure date was getting close, but I still had no tickets. Finally, with only a week to go, the tickets arrived. Or should I say the ticket. It was a one-way passage from Washington D.C. to Warsaw. I couldn't believe it. They had confused Washington State with Washington D.C...It was way too late to make any changes so I decided to use my company Air Travel Card to book a flight from Seattle to JFK in New York and to use the ticket I had received from Poland to go to Warsaw. That would take care of that problem. But wait a minute! This was only a one-way ticket! I was going behind the Iron Curtain on a one-way ticket...That sounded like a recipe for disaster...

It was with a certain level of anxiety that I boarded that flight, in early May, and headed for JFK International in New York. It was an airport that I would learn like the back of my hand in subsequent years. The flight was uneventful and sometime after 5:00 p.m. I arrived at the domestic terminal. The original terminal at JFK had been converted to the International Terminal, which was next to the new domestic terminal, so I walked over and tried to find my flight. I looked through the normal listing of Pan Am and TWA flights, but I could not find it. Finally, I located the flight near the bottom of the board. The airline was LOT. As I was to discover, it was the Polish Airline. "Hmmmm", I thought to myself, and I proceeded to the gate. I arrived at the gate and stared out the plate glass windows at the ramp, expecting to see a

Boeing 747 or perhaps a Lockheed L1011. Might heart sunk…There stood my flight. There was something totally bizarre about this aircraft. I could not recognize it immediately. My first impression was that the exterior of the fuselage was dirty, with streaks of oil visible.

I had been an aircraft enthusiast all my life. I made models as a kid of World War II aircraft and had an amazing collection of over 200 Wings aircraft cards which I had accumulated, little by little, by buying packages of bubble gum. In college I had been in the Air Force ROTC and had majored in aeronautical engineering. I had even worked for a summer at North American Aviation in Los Angeles as an engineering draftsman on the X-15 Rocket Plane, the fastest aircraft in the world. But this one had me stumped. There was something that worried me. This strange, four-engined aircraft with a huge "T" tail looked like something from another planet. Was this thing safe? Wasn't there something I remembered about a crash? I stared at the aircraft for what seemed an eternity. I couldn't quite put all the pieces together…

Then it hit me…It was a Russian Ilyushin-62 Intercontinental Transport. And there was a crash. Only 6 weeks earlier on March 14th this very same flight, LOT 007, was on final approach to runway 155 in Warsaw when the flight crew initiated an "overshoot" procedure. There was a problem with the locking of the landing gear so the crew had increased power to "go around". When power was increased, the number two engine had disintegrated. Debris from the number two engine, moving with the speed of an exploding artillery shell, damaged the rudder and control lines and the number three engine, causing the Ilyushin to enter an uncontrolled descent. The aircraft struck the ground in a twenty degree nose-down attitude and exploded, killing all 87 people on board, including members of the U.S. Amateur Boxing Team. When their bodies were autopsied, it was discovered that many on the team had held on their seats so strongly that, on impact, the muscles and tendons in their arms had been severed. They had obviously been aware they were going to crash.

As Wikipedia later reported: "After 26 seconds of uncontrolled descent, the aircraft clipped a tree with its right wing and impacted the ice-covered moat of a 19th-century military fortress with the speed of about 380 km/h (238 mph) at a 20-degree down angle, 950 meters away from the runway threshold and 100 meters from a residential area. At the last moment Captain Paweł Lipowczan, using nothing but the plane's ailerons, managed to avoid hitting a correctional facility for teenagers located at Rozwojowa street. On impact, the aircraft disintegrated; a large part of the main fuselage submerged in the moat, while the tail and parts of the main landing gear landed a few meters further, just before the entrance to the fort. The body of Captain Lipowczan was found lying on the street about sixty meters from the crash site; other bodies were scattered between the plane parts. On Capt. Lipowczan's right hand, small wounds were found, and they were confirmed to be made while Lipowczan was still alive; supposedly, he ripped the security off and tried to control the vertical trim, but it was too late".

Grim words…The engine that had exploded was a Russian, Kuznetsov NK-8-4 turbofan which turned out to have had serious vibration problems when installed on at least two other IL-62's. In order to save money, LOT had switched the engine from aircraft to aircraft with the bizarre rationale that, if it failed, at least there would be three other good engines to keep the plane aloft. No one ever envisioned that one disintegrating low pressure turbine fan could destroy two engines, the rudder, and the control cables. On analysis, the Poles determined "metal fatigue" to be the problem. When confronted with the evidence, the Russians denied it. However, it was later discovered, after the accident, that the Russians had secretly replaced all of the engines on their Ilyushin 62's with an upgraded model.

I stared out the window. The Iluyshin-62 sitting at the gate was named after Nicholas Copernicus, identical to the one that had crashed 6 weeks earlier. This was not a good sign…I stood there and tried to analyze my feelings… Suddenly, I was startled out of my reverie by the arrival of Dick, the Honeywell software engineer who had just arrived on a flight from Phoenix. We greeted each other, ordered a drink, and spent some time discussing the latest "inside baseball" Honeywell topics. It was a great relief to have something else to think about.

Finally, it was time to board. This was no Pan Am cruiser…The insides of the Ilyushin 62 were as dirty as the outsides, with an olive drab motif that made me think it might have been, at one time, a military aircraft. The seat backs had what appeared to be cargo netting to retain the non-existent magazines. This was certainly going to be a "no frills" flight, I thought to myself. I took my seat and fastened my seatbelt. I could hear the whine of the engines as they slowly spun up… We moved away from the gate and took our place on the taxiway. There was never an easy exit from JFK and this would be no exception. All wide bodies departed at approximately the same time in the evening, bound for Europe, so we took our place in line and slowly inched closer to the end of the runway. Finally it was our turn.

The engines went to full power and we accelerated down the runway. It seemed like an awfully long takeoff roll to me, but eventually we reached rotation speed. The nose lifted and we were off. Sort of…We did not climb out as I expected. Engine power was reduced and we slowly gained altitude. I began to wonder if this was some sort of fuel-saving initiative. Half an hour later we were still climbing with our seat belts on. Then I heard the whine of hydraulic motors and a "thunk". It sounded suspiciously like we had just raised the landing gear. I couldn't believe it. Normally the gear is raised immediately upon lift-off…I was beginning to lose confidence in this whole operation: at least what little confidence I had left…

Finally the seat belt sign was turned off. I looked out the window but it was too dark to make out any details. I unfastened my seat belt and walked down the aisle toward the back of the plane. I found the restroom and opened the door. The smell almost knocked me over. Obviously it had not been cleaned in an eternity… This was going to be a long trip.

Finally the cocktail service started. After a few beers I was feeling much more mellow. The meal was up to standards so I relaxed for a few minutes. I was not sitting with the software engineer, Dick, so I read my book for a while, walking up and down the aisles periodically to keep the blood circulating. Finally, the lights were dimmed and we settled down for the night, which was unfortunately very short.

Traveling East, morning always arrives in the middle of the night, so, like it or not, we prepared to begin a new day. I washed my hands and face, brushed my teeth and settled down to breakfast. After breakfast, I wandered about the cabin. I happened across a Polish woman who had been living in the States and spoke perfect English. She asked about where I was going in Poland and I told her that, according to my ticket, we were headed to Bydgoszcz, which, she explained, was pronounced "Bid-Goes". I thanked her for the pronunciation tip. She was very familiar with Bydgoszcz, so she asked about my hotel accommodations. I had no idea, so she took the opportunity to recommend the Brda hotel in the downtown area. I made a mental note of the name. It was pleasant to chat with someone in English and it passed the time away.

Then the engine noise suddenly began to subside. I looked at my watch and determined that we were about to land, so I returned to my seat. Moments later the seat belt sign turned on and I buckled up. As we descended, I looked out the window at the scenery. Time passed. The loudspeaker came to life: "Please collect your belongings. We are on final approach to Warsaw"…."Final Approach"…The words jarred me…We were now at the very spot that, just six weeks ago had been the grave site of LOT 007. How "final" was this approach going to be? Suddenly, my attention focused on a black-haired Polish man of slight build across the aisle. His face was white as a sheet. He appeared to be in a state of high anxiety and was "crossing himself" with a religious fervor that was terrifying… I couldn't help but think; did he know something that I didn't?

My thoughts were interrupted by the sound of hydraulic motors lowering the landing gear. This was it…The wheels touched with a squeal and we braked smoothly, taxiing to the end of the runway. WHEW! I breathed a sigh of relief. And then we stopped…

Why were we stopping? I looked out the window. I could see WARSZAWA clearly on the terminal building, but there did not appear to be any jetways. This seemed odd. Warsaw was the capital city of Poland. Surely they had jetways..I waited…and waited. After what seemed like half an hour or so I saw a bus approaching. It looked like a military vehicle. It stopped. Armed soldiers got out. A boarding stairway was rolled up to the aircraft and we began, slowly, to de-plane.

At the bottom of the stairs soldiers examined our travel documents. I was later to learn that, in Communist countries, all airport security was handled by the military. Finally, we were ushered onto the bus and transported to the terminal. We stepped through the doorway of the terminal and headed for the baggage collection area. The first thing I noticed was the terrible smell. The odors from the restrooms in the basement of the terminal were wafting up the stairs. As I proceeded down the stairs to enter the restrooms the intensity increased to a sickening level. Trying not to breathe, I visited the restroom and returned, as rapidly as possible, to the baggage collection area. "Welcome to The Communist People's Republic of Poland", I thought to myself.

By this time Dick had managed to locate the baggage. All of his software was stored on a "disk pack", which consisted of a round stack of magnetic platters held together by a common spindle. The disk pack measured about one foot in diameter and several inches thick and held about one million words of data, approximately 1/4000 of the data storage you could hold in the palm of your hand today. But these were different times…The magnetic platters were protected by a thick blue plastic cover. "We are never going to get this thing through customs", I thought to myself, "They're going to be all over us"…

But Dick did the right thing…He managed to hire a local Polish man standing around the baggage area to help us. Getting around the

Communist system, it turned out, usually involved knowing someone "on the inside" who could "grease the skids" for you, for a price…The man was excellent at his job, it turned out, and after much gesticulating and loud talk, he convinced the customs agent to let us through. We rolled our luggage cart into the main terminal area, which looked out upon the streets of Warsaw.

Now what? It was 9:30 in the morning. Our flight to Bydgoszcz was not until 3:00 p.m. We stored our luggage and walked out onto the street. Dick wanted to go downtown to see Warsaw, so we took the only available transit, which turned out to be an antiquated trolley car similar to one I had seen in World War II movies. It moved very slowly, stopping often. Forty five minutes later, we were in the Old Town section of Warsaw and we exited the tram. We looked around… In the Soviet Era, Poland was desperately poor, as were all Communist countries. I would come to appreciate the full magnitude of the situation over the next two weeks. Today, however, we were just tourists.

I looked up. There before us was St. Anne's church. We moved towards it, entering the church and walking up the stairs to the Bell Tower. We could not read the signs or the historical information, but we were able to glean some insight from one of the docents who explained to us that St. Anne's was one of the only churches not damaged significantly by Nazi bombs in WWII. I was later to learn that the Nazi plan had been to totally destroy Warsaw and that they had very nearly been successful. The view from the Bell Tower was spectacular, with panoramic vistas of the city, totally rebuilt. In my mind's eye I recalled the black and white footage from WW II movies depicting the destruction of Warsaw… It had been almost complete. Today, the rebuilt city was displayed before me, risen like a Phoenix from the ashes. I was very impressed…but not for long…

We descended the stairs and exited onto the sidewalk. We had no idea where to go or what to do, so we just walked, staring up at the buildings and taking in the sights. And that was how we discovered the

Palace of Culture. This was the most peculiar building that I had ever seen in my life, very tall with huge Gothic spires and turrets. As we approached the building, we discovered that it was a museum. Perfect. We had more time on our hands so we went in.

As I was to discover later, this bizarre architecture was referred to as "Stalinesque", after Joseph Stalin, who insisted upon enforcing it as a design code upon all new structures built within the USSR and satellite countries. As it turned out, the Palace of Culture, with its impossible grotesque spires was a "present" from Stalin to the People of Poland. I couldn't imagine the celebration that the Polish people must have had to endure when the building was dedicated. Later, I was to find out that, when no one was listening, people across the USSR referred to these buildings as "Stalins' Wedding Cakes". That made perfect sense.

And so we entered the Palace of Culture. But we were not allowed up the stairs. First, we had to pay the admittance fee of 15 Zlotys, and then we had to "check our coats" in the checkroom before we were allowed to proceed. The museum was upstairs, so we walked up to the second floor and entered the premises. Unfortunately, it was impossible to read any of the information presented, so we were pretty much on our own to figure out what we were looking at. Nothing made sense. I took my time…"No, this couldn't be", I thought to myself, so I looked some more. Finally, I could no longer ignore the evidence. THIS WAS A VACUUM CLEANER MUSEUM! So much for the delights of Communism and Stalin's Palace of Culture…We got our coats back from the checkroom and exited the building.

I was concerned that we might have some difficulty boarding our flight to Bydgoszcz, so we found the street car and returned to the airport. We recovered our luggage and headed to the gate. I was now becoming extremely wary of Soviet aircraft so I looked this one over pretty carefully. I could not tell what it was. It looked like a Soviet copy of the Fokker F-27 high-wing twin turboprop regional aircraft that I hated. Because the fuselage was suspended below the wings it had a sickening tendency to roll side-to-side like a pendulum in rough air. I was just going to have to make the best of it…

Finally, the flight was called. We exited the terminal, walking across the ramp and climbed the boarding stairs. The flight was full and the interior was somewhat cramped so I took my seat and stared out the window. Soon we were in the air and headed towards Bydgoszcz. The flight was somewhat longer than I expected, but after an hour or so in the air, the runway was in site. We circled the field and descended, but our landing speed and rate of descent were abnormally high. We hit the field hot and hard and braked to a stop. I thought for sure that we must have a military pilot.

And then the taxiing began. We taxied and we taxied and still, we taxied. The pilot had slammed the plane down on the very end of the runway and brought it to a halt, apparently not realizing that the passengers had to deplane at the far end of the runway. So he taxied some more. Finally, we arrived at the far end of the runway and I could exit the aircraft.

I descended the boarding stairs. At last I was on firm ground. I looked around. Where was the terminal? There was none. Where was the person that was supposed to meet us? I could not really process this. The sun was going down and I hadn't had any sleep in two days. Baggage and tools were being unloaded on the ground and people were picking up their possessions and walking away. Now there was no one left but Dick and myself. The last rays of the sun were shining over the embankment above the runway and we were in deep shadow. There had been four or five buses parked there but now there was only one.

"What are we going to do?" Dick asked, "I don't know", I said, "But there's only one bus left and we'd better be on it". We scrambled up the embankment with our luggage and climbed aboard. The driver looked at me questioningly. All I could remember from my conversation with the Polish woman on the plane was the hotel recommendation. "Brda" I said, hoping for the best. The driver seemed to understand and in a few minutes we found ourselves stopping at what seemed to be an old but decent hotel.

We could not communicate with the desk clerk but, luckily, rooms were available so we got our assignments, grabbed our luggage and headed upstairs. I think we ate dinner that night, but I was so tired I have no recollection of it. There was one thing, however, that we agreed upon; there was absolutely no way we could deal with our situation that night. We made a plan to attack it in the morning, after a good night's sleep, which we sorely needed.

The next morning I tapped on Dick's door. What the heck were we going to do? Dick had a telephone in the room, but neither of us could speak Polish…We had to try something. We looked at the phone… It had no dial or buttons…We would have to communicate by voice. Hmmmm…The only information that been provided to us was the name of the chemical company, Zaklady Chemiczne, and the city, which was Inowroclaw, pronounced "EnoVrutzWuff" as close as I could remember.

I picked up the phone and listened. Someone answered. My mind flashed back thirty years to my childhood in New Jersey. Our telephone had no numbers or buttons then, so when we picked up the handset an operator would inquire, "Number please!" But I had no number to give them. All I could do was give them the city. "EnoVrutzWuff" I said as clearly as possible into the phone.

Amazingly enough, it worked, and after a short pause I heard an operator say, "EnoVrutzWuff". Wow! I couldn't believe it. This system apparently pre-dated the self-dialing or even the telephone numbering system. It seemed to rely on operators in each city who would connect your call by name rather than number.

This might work…The Inowroclaw operator had answered. Boldly, I spoke into the phone, "Zaklady Chemiczne", the name of the chemical company. There was a brief pause and then I heard the operator at the chemical company pick up. "Zaklady Chemiczne", she said. Now what?…I racked my brain…The only person we knew from the chemical company was the engineer who had attended the Honeywell training school in Phoenix. His name was Wychek.

I went for it…"WeeChek", I said carefully into the phone. My luck ran out. I heard a babble of Polish. I couldn't understand a word. My frustration level was through the roof. No one spoke English. No one knew where we were or could help us. Dick intervened. "Let's just go down and have some breakfast and think about this", he said. I agreed.

The breakfast was agreeably good, and I even think we had fresh strawberries. The coffee was beginning to energize my brain. I relaxed. Dick looked at me. "You know," he said thoughtfully, "I think, in Polish, that a 'W' is pronounced as a 'V', which means that his name is pronounced 'VeeChek'". We finished breakfast and headed back to Dick's room. I was going to try this one more time.

I picked up the phone and asked for Inowroclaw. The Inowroclaw operator answered. I gave them the name of the chemical company and the Zaklady Chemiczne operator picked up. Carefully I pronounced "VeeChek" into the phone, hoping for the best. IT WORKED! Suddenly Wychek was on the phone asking us where the heck we were…I was overjoyed…Luckily, he had been standing next to the operator, checking on our flight arrivals when I called. We told him about the hotel and our difficulties. He apologized. I could tell he was very upset. As I was later to discover, there was a certain person in Phoenix in charge of travel arrangements who always "added one day" to the arrival date of anyone traveling overseas, thinking he was compensating for the "time difference". I knew who that person was…I could have killed him…

Wychek immediately put together a plan and several hours later, a van arrived to transport us to our new "digs" in a better neighborhood: the old medieval town of Torun. It was a Friday, and the plan had been for us to recover from our overseas flight and then report to work on Monday. I appreciated their thoughtfulness. The town was ancient but beautiful in a very old-fashioned way. As I was to learn, it was one of the oldest cities in Poland, built around 1200 A.D. and one of its scenic wonders. It had successfully escaped destruction by the Nazi's during WWII. In the Old Town area, ancient walls protected the gothic buildings. It was known today as a "university town", after the university that was established in 1945.

The hotel had seen better days, but was quite adequate. There was a single bed in my room covered with nothing but a down comforter which was warm and very soft. I slept late into the morning, but not completely by design. I had cleverly plugged my clock into a voltage converter so that it operated on 120 VAC. But what I had failed to recognize was that the power was 50 cycles instead of 60 cycles, so that every hour the clock ran, it lost 10 minutes. I checked my LCD watch and was shocked to see that it was actually 10:30 a.m. and not 8:00, as my clock said.

I went down for a late breakfast and looked around. Dick was nowhere in sight, so sat down in the restaurant and looked at the menu. There were some English translations below the items, so I could make out the basic offerings. The waitress spoke limited English also, which I appreciated. "Coffee or juice?" she asked me. No one had ever asked me to make a choice before, so I selected "coffee". Several minutes later, the coffee arrived…Apparently the method for making coffee was to stir coffee grounds into an individual cup of hot water and then to serve it with grounds floating on top…This was not a Starbuck's kind of place…

I had not yet begun to appreciate the devastating effect that Communism had on the people of Poland. There was a food shortage everywhere which, at first, had not been obvious to me. When I went to dinner the night before, the waiter had presented me with a large menu consisting of several pages. I was delighted. I tried to order the chicken. "No, No", the waiter said "Fini", which I took to mean "finished" or "not available". I went down the menu. Each item that I asked for would be "Fini". Finally, I asked the waiter what he would recommend. He pointed to the only thing available, "Bifstek", which I took to mean "beef steak".

Now this was not your Ruth's Chris Steak House kind of steak. This one was, as the menu clearly stated, "100 grams", or three and one-half ounces, barely enough to cover the inside palm of your hand. It came with a few root vegetables, which were very commonly grown in the cold northern climate. In some years the short growing season never materialized at all, causing severe rationing. Luckily, the beer was plentiful and not all that bad...

And so it was on this particular Saturday morning that I finished breakfast and walked out the door of the hotel...And I ran into my first drunk, staggering across the lawn with a bottle in his hand. I couldn't believe it. This early in the morning? It was culture shock. I was a slow learner, but gradually I pieced together some of the basic tenets of life under Communism. Basically, there were three things guaranteed to every citizen: full employment, a place to live, and, last but not least, cheap vodka, made, of course, from the main root vegetable, the potato.

Collective farms produced little food, without the incentive of the free market system and the private sector was non-existent, so there was very little wealth in the country or any of the Soviet countries. The only entertainment available was drinking vodka, which was indulged in quite heavily. In Russian restaurants, as I was to discover, waiters appeared in the middle of meals, going from table to table with huge trays of glasses filled to the brim with a clear liquid. When I asked about it, the waiter replied, somewhat annoyed, "It is your vodka ration!". Apparently, the only way to tolerate life under Communism was to anesthetize yourself, and as frequently as possible.

I headed down towards the Old City. As I turned a corner, I discovered a parade in progress with brass bands and women dressed in peasant costumes. I followed it to the town square, where wreaths were being laid at the base of a large statue. I stood by and watched for a while, until the crowd had dissipated. I was sure that the Soviets would not let the Poles celebrate any of their more radical national political heroes, so I was curious as to the identity of this statue. When everyone had gone, I walked to the base and looked up. It was the statue of Nicolaus Copernicus.

I was shocked...It was also the name of the Iluyshin-62 that I had flown across the Atlantic, as well as the name of the Iluyshin-62 that had crashed. In fact, as I was to learn later, LOT had named all of their IL-62's "Nicolaus Copernicus". And as it turned out, the village of Torun had been his birthplace in 1473. Copernicus was the first medieval astronomer to postulate a heliocentric system, displacing the theory that the earth was the center of the universe. That must have created quite a stir back in those days, but to celebrate it 500 years later seemed totally anachronistic...Or maybe it was just a political reality...

I continued my walk. As I proceeded further, I noticed an odd tree-lined ravine, right in the center of town. I couldn't quite make out the structures behind the trees but they appeared to be part of a military fortification. Suddenly, I heard a shout. I looked up...A line of Soviet troops was moving out from the ravine onto the city streets. There was not doubt about their purpose, which was to remind the population that this was no longer their country but a piece of a larger puzzle known as the USSR; "... a riddle, wrapped in a mystery, inside an enigma" as Winston Churchill had characterized it. As I got closer, I could see that they were just youths, 17 or 18 years of age and they were engaging in typical teenage horseplay. The only difference was, they were carrying automatic weapons...I began walking in the other direction.

Sunday passed uneventfully. I decided to go for a run along the Vistula River, which was a short distance away. As I approached the river, I noticed a long, grass-covered embankment with a concrete pathway disappearing in the distance. "Perfect", I thought to myself. It was a beautiful day...I began to jog...the miles passed effortlessly. Up ahead I could see an elderly woman walking in the middle of the path. As I approached, she heard my footsteps and turned around with the most fearful expression that I have ever seen. Her fear penetrated me like a knife. In her eyes I could see the terror of World War II and the brutality of the Nazis. Three thousand Poles a day had died during the Nazi occupation. It was a sobering moment...Maybe running was not such a great idea...I returned to the hotel, shaken by the experience.

The next morning was Monday, our first day of work. The van arrived at 7:30 a.m. sharp and we climbed aboard for our ride to Inowroclaw and the chemical plant. The ride was unremarkable and I stared out the window at the passing scenery. We stopped at a railroad crossing. I waited in anticipation of seeing a train cross in front of us. Nothing happened. We waited for about 10 minutes. Finally the train passed and the crossing gate lifted. My curiosity was piqued; what kind of automation system would bring down the crossing gate 10 minutes before the train arrived? As the bus crossed over the tracks, I looked down at the crossing gate mechanism. I could see that the gate was run by a manual cable of some sort. As we proceeded forward, I traced the path of the cable under the tracks and up the side of a building. There on the top of the building was an operator cranking a large cable drum! I couldn't believe my eyes...Later I was to learn that many fatalities in Poland were caused by the operator getting drunk and failing to lower the crossing gate in time. This operator had obviously decided to err on the side of caution...

We continued on our journey to the plant. We entered the control room and were introduced to all of the personnel, most of whom had been trained at Honeywell in Phoenix and who spoke English very well. We talked about our trip and our plans for the site. Finally, the pleasantries were over and we entered the computer room to assess the situation. We reviewed the documentation and looked at the arrangement of the equipment, which had already been emplaced.

Things were proceeding as anticipated. After days of alien experiences, I was at last getting down to something I knew very well. I opened computer cabinets and inspected the hardware. After a while, I began to notice that my vision was becoming somewhat blurry. If I blinked rapidly, I could momentarily clear my eyes…And then my eyes began to sting so badly that I could not continue. I became aware of the smell of ammonia. It takes only a few parts-per-million of ammonia to irritate the eyes and the nasal passages, but this concentration far exceeded the threshold. It was an emergency situation. Our hosts entered the room. "There has been an ammonia leak", they told us. By this time the concentration was so intense that it was getting difficult to breathe. "Let's just go into the hallway", they said. "The concentration is not so strong". We stood in the hallway…The odor was somewhat better but, only momentarily. Soon the concentration of ammonia in the hallway was worse than in the computer room. I noticed a gas mask on the wall. "Can I use the gas mask?" I asked our hosts. "Yes", they said, so quickly I donned what I can only describe as a World War II gas mask with full face coverage, large glass lenses, and a filter canister sticking out in front. I had come all this way to work on the computer and I was damned if I was going to let this situation stop me from doing my work and returning to the U.S. …and the sooner, the better…

I re-entered the computer room and stared into the cabinet. Quickly, I realized that I did not have sufficient vision, through the gas mask, to really see what I was doing. Before I could analyze the situation any further, my host tapped me on the shoulder. "We are going to lunch now". Apparently I had totally embarrassed my hosts and they were attempting to do everything possible to distract me from the situation. I acquiesced.

I was concerned. It was a well known trick of the Soviets to move the manufacturing of military supplies and munitions to the satellite countries, where they could obtain Western goods and support. I suspected that this plant was manufacturing military-grade explosives for the USSR. I knew that the main component of conventional explosives was nitrogen, which was also the main component of ammonia. I was worried that we were working in a "powder plant" or something even worse.

I had had some experience with explosives and powder plants. Back in the 'sixties, I had taken over a contract for Honeywell in DuPont, Washington named after the DuPont Chemical Company. When I drove out to the site, I wondered at the different structures, all hidden away in a woodland. When I asked about this, the engineer at the administration building told me, in a manner-of-fact way, that all the buildings were separated so that if one blew up it would not destroy all the others. Great…

It was not without some fear that I approached the building at DuPont housing the Honeywell temperature and moisture recorder. I entered the front door…There, in the middle of the room was a huge vat, being slowly stirred by a gigantic mixing blade. The whole back of the room was missing. "Why is the wall missing back there?" I asked naively. "Because, they explained, "if the vat explodes it will just blow out the back". "Oh" I said.

So I began to calibrate the recorder. "What if I get this thing wrong?" I thought to myself. I continued my work. Finally, I got up enough courage to ask the operator. "What happens if the moisture level is not correct?" "Well" it depends, he said, adding some water to the mix. "If I let this thing get too dry, then it will explode". "Uh-oh" I thought to myself. I stared at the chart on the front of the instrument. I had done my best to calibrate it properly, but there was really no way to confirm the accuracy of the moisture level of the mix. I did notice, however, that the pen indicating the moisture level on the chart was not inking properly. "I'll just get another pen from the car", I said to myself, glad for the chance to get away from the building, if only for a moment.

I walked to my car and opened the trunk. I was sorting through my parts when it happened. BOOM! An explosion so loud that it took by breath away. I could feel the shock wave pass through my body. My ears were ringing. My worst fears had come true. I looked around. I could see that the building was still standing. I approached the door with great trepidation. I opened it and looked inside…Everything appeared normal. How could this be?

"What was that?" I asked. "What?" the operator asked. "That explosion", I said…"Oh", he replied, that was just an artillery shell". "What do you mean?" I asked incredulously. Then he pointed to a trestle that I could barely make out through the trees. "We have to test every batch of artillery shells, so we send one out on that trestle over the ravine and explode it ever so often". My nervous system was in a state of near collapse…I thanked the operator for the information and finished up, writing my report as rapidly as possible before the next shell went off.

And so it was with great relief that I pulled off my gas mask at Zaklady Chemiczne and joined the others for lunch. We drove off, escaping from the ammonia cloud. Our driver stopped at a nearby restaurant and got out, but he motioned for us to stay in the car. He returned. The restaurant was closed. There was no food. He tried a second restaurant…Still no luck. Even a third restaurant…nothing. At last, he hit upon a restaurant that, by some miracle had managed to get enough food to open. We all sat around a large table and ordered our meals.

It was very pleasant. Our hosts were very concerned about our welfare, which we appreciated. They had all been to Honeywell classes in Phoenix, so we traded stories. We laughed about the language difficulties. They could not understand why Burger King would not sell them a hamburger for breakfast. And then one of them explained about trying to buy food at a restaurant to take back to the hotel. The waitress looked at them blankly. "To bring away", they tried to explain…The waitress looked puzzled. They tried every word that they could think of in English to describe what they wanted. Finally, they all came to an understanding. It was TAKEOUT they wanted…Everyone laughed…

I couldn't resist it…I know I shouldn't have done it…but it was too late… I had to ask them. Polish Jokes were becoming very popular back in the

States. Now I had to find out what nationality the Poles told their jokes about. It wasn't long before I found out. "We tell jokes on Scottish persons", they exclaimed. And then they proceeded to tell a Scottish joke. "There was this Scottish person", they related, "who walked up to a farmer and asked about the price of honey. The farmer told him the price". Our host paused for effect. "And then the Scottish person asked, 'Well how much is the price for one bee'?" They all cracked up. Then they asked the question that I was afraid they were going to ask. "Who do you tell jokes about?" they enquired. I fumbled the ball, but Dick came to my rescue. "Italians", he said. I was relieved to get out of that one.

When lunch was over we returned to the site and found that the ammonia leak had been plugged and the gas cloud had dissipated. We resumed our efforts and proceeded, at last, to make some progress installing the computer system. Slowly, we fell into a routine and the days passed quickly. I worked up the courage to ask the waitress in the hotel for both coffee AND juice, which caused some sort of minor crisis. The waitress was shocked and I could here her relating the story to the other employees. I could only imagine what she was saying about the bourgeois American who was ordering such an extravagant meal. She came back and informed me that "there would be an extra charge", hoping to dissuade me. But I held my ground. I received a coffee, a small glass of juice, my breakfast and a bill: for U.S. $7.00.

But the worst thing was the toilet paper. It was kind of an un-bleached, brown crepe paper, as best as I could describe, and very rough…There was only a very small roll supplied…and it was not re-supplied. I had to wait until the weekend to wave an empty roll at the cleaning lady in order to get a refill. I remember rationing in World War II but nothing was this bad. I would come to understand the problem later as I observed a logging operation in a forest in northern Poland.

But the weekend was now upon us. Dick and I tried to put together a plan. I noticed a small theater in town that was playing an American movie: Straight Time with Dustin Hoffman. I assumed that the sub-titles would be in Polish but that the English would be under-standable, so we went to the box office to purchase the tickets. But, it was not so simple…It appeared that we had to have an advanced reser-vation and an assigned seat. We opted for the next showing, purchased our tickets, and returned several hours later. We walked upstairs and found ourselves in a large room, similar to a high school gymnasium with folding chairs, arranged in straight lines with no center aisles. We scooted down the long row and took our assigned seats. In the front of the room there was a small screen that rolled down from the ceiling. IMAX this was not.

Then the show started. I had puzzled over the selection of the movie. Of all of the American movies available, why had the Soviets allowed this particular one to be shown? I suspected that only movies depict-ing Americans in a bad light would be selected, and I was right. The plot revolved around the American justice system and the fact that Dustin Hoffman's parole officer was totally corrupt. In the middle of the movie, the parole officer tells a Polish Joke. "Did you hear about the Pollock who got third degree burns of the face?" "No", says the Dustin Hoffman character. "He was dunking for French fries", replies the officer. Just as I started to laugh, I caught myself. I looked around… Everyone was staring seriously at the screen…No one made a noise. Apparently the joke had not been translated into Polish…Either that or the people were taking great offense…I choked back my laughter…

But then the most incredible thing happened, which, in my mind, was to make a mockery of Communism and its attempt to control the minds of the Polish people. There, in a later scene in the movie, the Dustin Hoffman character is seen visiting the home of a small time hoodlum in Los Angeles. To me it was unremarkable, but when the two characters sat down next to a pool in the back yard, the entire audi-ence burst out into an "AHHHHHHH". I could not understand it at first… Then it hit me…Here was a poor man, a small time criminal in an evil, Capitalist bourgeois society…But even he could afford a house with A SWIMMING POOL…My heart leapt with joy…

Now it was Sunday. Dick had been thinking upon a plan for days and now he wanted to execute it. It turned out to be a far more grandiose than any of the plans that I had conceived. In fact, I was little taken aback by the boldness of it. Dick was proposing that we visit the ancient seaport of Gdansk on the Baltic Sea, a "free city" that had been designated "Danzig" by the German population of Poland under the terms of the Versailles Treaty. After World War II the Germans in the city had been either deported or expelled and the name had been restored to "Gdansk". Either way, it was a fair distance from Torun. The Communist system had given both Dick and I a certain reluctance to trust the government, so this trip was more about finding an "escape route" from Poland should we need to take it. We knew that ferries at the seaport could take us across the Baltic to "neutral" countries, such as Sweden should that be required. In Dick's case this became a premonition of things to come…

We stood at the train station looking at the schedules. Gdansk was a popular destination and trains departed fairly frequently. We purchased tickets and waited. It took some detective work to determine the platform on which the train was to arrive, but eventually we found it, boarded and took our seats. It was a going to be a long ride, but the trip ended in Gdansk, so there was no way we could miss our final destination. I stared out the window. The countryside moved past and I spent time looking at farmer's fields and forests. The girl across the aisle from me was reading a book that looked extremely dull. The book itself had faded beige cover with a typeset that reminded me of something out of the 19th century. I could make out the word "Socialism" on the front cover. This was obviously required reading. The girl looked extremely bored with the entire subject. Slowly, the book dropped to her lap and she dozed off.

I looked at the forests. To me they were not forests at all but pre-planted "plantations" of spindly trees no more than two inches in diameter. Shortly, we came across a logging camp. I couldn't believe it. They were actually logging these trees…I thought they were just immature trees waiting to grow up, but apparently they were large enough for harvesting. There was no way to make lumber out of these matchsticks, so they must have been destined for the pulp mills to be used for paper. No wonder the toilet paper was so low in quality…Poland apparently had only limited resources of natural forests. Now I understood why European visitors to the United States would marvel at our use of tree trunks for telephone poles…Throughout Europe all light standards, telephone poles and guard rails were made of metal…

Finally, we arrived at the station in Gdansk. Unfortunately, as we discovered, the train station was several miles from the seaport, so we decided to walk. It took us over two hours to walk the distance and my Western boots were killing me… We stood on top of an embankment and looked at the Lenin Shipyards, re-named by the Soviets for the Father of Communism. Little did we know that in only three short months, on August 14th, 1980, Lech Walesa would stand on this very spot, joining the general shipyard strike and demanding freedom for Poland. His Solidarity movement, only nine years later, would carry him to the office of President, where he would preside over the transition of Poland from a Communist to a Democratic state. We were on hallowed ground…

Walking back was a killer. We stopped at a restaurant along the way and were un-surprised to learn that "bifstek" was going to be our dinner choice… We really didn't care…We would have done anything to be able to sit down, get off our feet and have a few beers. Refreshed, we walked back to the station. We had not been permitted to purchase round trip tickets so we had to negotiate for a one way return. It was getting dark and we hoped that we could reserve some sort of compartment. No such luck… Most of the compartments were full, so we opted for an "option" ticket which gave us the right to enter a compartment if space were available. We searched all the cars…people were stuffed into every compartment and were fast asleep, so we retreated to the lower cost seating area. The ride was uneventful, except, of course for the rowdy soldiers drinking beer and making a commotion. It had been easy getting to a main hub like Gdansk in Poland, but it was not so easy returning. We had to look out the windows at every stop to determine if this were the right one. In the dark, it was hard to see the signs, but, eventually we identified the stop at Torun, got off the train and walked back to our hotel. What a day…

I was worried. We were now entering our second week on site and I had not yet received my return ticket. I mentioned frequently to our hosts that I needed passage back to Seattle at the end of the week, as we had agreed upon. By law, Polish visas were explicitly written for "day of entry" and "day of departure". Any deviation from these dates resulted in a revocation of the visa and possible criminal penalties, not to mention the extreme difficulty of obtaining a new visa. In Japan, a relative of my wife, a student, had been imprisoned for overstaying his visa by just one day. Everyone on site was polite, but still no ticket. I was hoping that our hosts could help turn the cogs of the Communist government just a little faster, but so far we were at a dead stop. Time was running out. The computer system was up and running and had passed all of the diagnostic tests. I was ready to go. Dick was planning to stay on site after I left to complete the software installation and certification and begin the warranty period.

It was Tuesday. Our trip to the site started off normally, but the new driver apparently lost the way. Suddenly, we found ourselves looking out at a vast field of rubble that had once been Inowroclaw's industrial area. Our driver apologized profusely…He had not wanted us to see the damage wrought by Allied and Soviet bombers during the war, but there it was in plain sight. Before we could get a good look, the driver pulled away. Our hosts had wanted, above all, to protect us from the unseemly side of Poland. It didn't seem to be working…

But still no ticket… It was now Wednesday of the second week and the government had not been forthcoming. Wychek made a plan. He would accompany me all the way to Warsaw in the van and personally go to the government agencies necessary to generate the ticket. I was very appreciative. It would be a good chance to talk to Wychek about the real nature of Communism in Poland. It was very important to Wychek that Dick and I leave with a good impression of Poland, so he invited us over to his father's house for dinner. Wychek's mother had died some time ago, but his father had gone to great efforts to prepare a delicious dinner for the four of us. His father had survived World War II and was very grateful to Americans for lifting the Nazi curse. We thanked him profusely and left feeling extremely appreciated.

Thursday came and I said goodbye to Dick. I was very relieved to have some assistance getting out of Poland. When Wychek arrived I was waiting on the curb. I climbed into the van and we started our long and tortuous ride to Warsaw, a trip that was to take about three to four hours. This van was no Lincoln Navigator. The springs were bad, the seat cushioning was minimal and the road noise was high. The highways were not the best, so it was a somewhat challenging ride, but I didn't really care. I was going home, hopefully all the way to Seattle and not the other Washington…

The road improved somewhat as the hours passed, so I had a chance to ask Wychek some questions about living in a Communist State. First, I asked him about the numerous signs, painted in bright yellow letters on a red Communist background. They seemed to exist everywhere. They were the Burma Shave signs of Poland. "They are slogans", he replied. I asked him to translate some but he dismissed them out of hand. I could tell he didn't wasn't to talk about the Communist influence. In the van we had some privacy. The driver could not understand English, so Wychek could talk without being overhead. Despite the ideal conditions, however, Wychek held his cards close to his vest.

Then I asked him about the private sector. "Oh yes, we have one", he said. "In fact my wife runs a small business in the basement of our house building automobile speedometers". "Oh", I said "Is that a good business?" "Yes", he said "but we cannot expand". When I asked him why, he replied: "Because, under Communism no private business can have more than three employees". I was shocked. "So much for the free enterprise system", I thought to myself. Finally, Wycheck warmed up to my questioning. "You know, I have to explain to you about our life". I was all ears. He started out; "In Poland, under Communism we have full employment". He paused for effect. "Yes", I said, "I understand". He continued; "But it does not matter whether you are horizontal or vertical". That was very funny...a Polish joke...but very true. Production was not important, only attendance. That probably explained why I had to hunt all over Torun for souvenirs to take home. There were practically no consumer goods available, so I had to settle for some colorful eggs, painted by peasants in the countryside. I wondered if they had more than three employees...

We were now arriving at the outskirts of Warsaw. This was going to be a lot more difficult than I thought. There did not appear to be much parking available, but, luckily, our driver could circle the block while we assaulted the Communist government agencies. We took the elevator up. This looked like a difficult case, but I could not really evaluate the proceedings. Wychek consulted with the administrators for several minutes. Finally, he was finished. But I still had no ticket. "We have to go to another agency", he informed me. We returned to the van and drove down the block.

We attacked the next agency. It was the same story. A brief consultation followed by a quick exit. Still no ticket. But the third time was the charm. After several minutes of conversation and a brief wait, the tickets miraculously appeared. Wychek had done an exceptional job... the tickets were from Warsaw to Seattle, Washington. I was overjoyed. On the one hand, I was very excited to be going home, but on the other, I was beginning to feel sorry for the people of Poland. Our jokes had mis-characterized them as stupid and inept. In truth, they were a very hard-working and intelligent people burdened with a Communist government that choked off their resources and prevented them from rising to the level of excellence that had characterized them in earlier generations. The Poles had been traumatized first by the Nazis and later by the Soviets, but it had not bent their will. In just three months, on that very spot that we visited only a week ago, Lech Walesa would begin the fight to lead this country out of Communism and into Democracy…

I was very appreciative of Wychek's efforts, but I had one favor to ask. I hoped he wouldn't mind. I really wanted to capture Warsaw as I saw it, but I had run out of film. I asked if he could find me some 35 mm. color film. He was very agreeable, and thus began our two and a half hour tour of Warsaw in search of something that was readily available in Western countries. But it was during this expedition that I began to see the real Poland. It was not the Old Town of Torun or the restored Old Town of Warsaw but the real Warsaw. Shops were empty of goods; visiting a grocery store, all I saw were wooden bins of dried food. We moved on. The streets were virtually empty of vehicles, with the exception of the Polski Fiats and the Russian "Trabbies", three-cylinder vehicles with two-stroke, 26 horsepower engines that were, arguably, the worst example of automotive engineering ever to grace this planet.

Wikipedia explained: "The **Trabant** was a car produced by former East German auto maker VEB Sachsenring Automobilwerke Zwickau. It was the most common vehicle in East Germany, and was also exported to countries both inside and outside the communist bloc. The main selling point was that it had room for four adults and luggage in a compact, light and durable shell. With its mediocre performance, inefficient two-stroke engine, noxious fumes and production shortages, the Trabant is often cited as an example of the disadvantages of Centralized Planning; on the other hand, it is regarded with derisive affection as a symbol of the failed former East Germany and of the fall of communism. Since it could take years for a Trabant to be delivered from the time it was ordered, people who finally got one were very careful with it and usually became skillful in maintaining and repairing it. The lifespan of an average Trabant was 28 years. Used Trabants would often fetch a higher price than new ones, as the former were available immediately, while the latter required the infamous long wait. It was in production without any significant changes for nearly 30 years with 3,096,099 Trabants manufactured in total. In 2008, Time magazine rated the Trabant as **one of the 50 worst cars ever made**".

We continued our quest. Upon locating a store that carried no 35 mm cartridges, Wychek would inquire as to where the film might be found. This led us on a wild goose chase through side streets and main boulevards. As frustrating as this shopping expedition was turning out to be, it was eye-opening as I began to see the real Poland under Communism. This was not the tourist section of Warsaw...I watched the people; most were shabbily dressed...There were military personnel everywhere. For every civilian walking in the street I saw at least one Soviet Army officer or enlisted man. Warsaw was beginning to look like a Soviet military base...

As we rounded a corner, I saw a long line of people, stretching around the block. They appeared to be queuing up in front of a window in the center of a large building. "What's happening over there?" I asked Wychek. "Oh", he said, "they're lining up for ice cream". Words failed me...All I could manage was an incredulous, "Ice cream?" Was this possible?...In Poland, it certainly was...I thought about it for a very long time afterwards...

And then we hit pay dirt...sort of...The newspaper store we visited did have 35 mm. film. There was only one problem...There was only one roll available and it and it was black and white. I hadn't shot black and white film since the early 'sixties, when I had my own developing and printing equipment. But somehow this seemed appropriate in Warsaw. Everything I saw around me was in shades of Communist gray. The buildings were gray, the roads were gray, the people were gray and the clothes were faded and unremarkable. Shooting color film would have been a waste of time. I suddenly focused on this remarkable absence of color. There were no McDonald's Golden Arches signs or any colorful signs whatsoever. It was a somber government society with no frills and no advertising. "Plain" does not begin to describe Warsaw under Communism in 1980.

And so it was that my day ended. I thanked Wychek for his kind-ness and checked into my hotel. I made sure to tell the desk that I needed a cab at 5:30 the next morning for my 8:30 departure from Warszawa-Okecie Airport. I was taking no chances. It was hard to sleep that night. I worried that the cab driver might not show up. But this was not South America…The driver showed up promptly at 5:30 and we were off….We arrived at the airport shortly thereafter.

I was not quite prepared for the intensive search that was to follow. The customs agents looked at my camera and asked if I had taken any pictures of bridges, train stations or airports. Wykchek had reminded me that it was illegal to photograph such structures and I had observed that regulation. "No", I told them. Then they went through every piece of my luggage. I had never heard of such a customs inspection when leaving the country. Usually it was only upon arrival that such searches were made. Then they found it…The only thing in Poland that I had found to purchase other than the eggs…About 100 Soviet and Polish postage stamps. The agent looked concerned. She took the stamps and departed to check with the Commisar. And I sat and waited…Was I going to be arrested, or interrogated? Would I miss my flight? Would my visa be revoked? Would I ever see the U.S. again? These thoughts raced through my mind…I knew that I had no civil rights in a for-eign country, and especially in this foreign country. Soviets hated the U.S….I could only wait…

The minutes ticked by…I had really liked these stamps. If there was one thing that the Soviets could do well it was to manufacture postage stamps. They spared no expense in making them colorful and attractive, commemorating everything from Sputnik to the Soviet Cosmonauts. It was an exceptionally powerful propaganda tool for them and it would make an ideal present for me to present to my father-in-law, Martin, who was a stamp collector.

I waited some more. Now I was getting a little agitated. Finally, the agent returned. She looked at me...My fate hung in the balance. "No problem", she said. I was relieved. I headed to the gate. I still had some Polish Zlotys in my pocket, but there was no way I could exchange them for U.S. dollars. No other country in the world would touch this currency. I would take it home as a souvenir.

I boarded the LOT Iluyshin-62 and took my seat, trying not to think about the flight into Warsaw. We taxied out to the runway and within minutes we were airborne. This was it…I was going home… We reached altitude and I began to relax. Suddenly, the engines slowed and we began to descend. Uh-oh…"This looks like trouble", I thought to myself.. I could feel the tension rising. Was there some sort of problem? I looked out the window…I could see a runway beneath us but I could not tell where we were. The plane touched down and rolled to a stop. I asked the flight attendant what we were doing. She explained that the Warsaw airport was out of jet fuel again and that we were stopping in Communist East Berlin to gas up. I looked out the window. There was a jack-booted military officer walking the perimeter with a German Shepherd… It was a chilling reminder of the Nazi SS.

I was sitting in the front row of the aircraft and the cockpit door was open. I could not understand the conversation that the pilot was having with the military officer on the ground, but I could read the body language. The pilot was overly deferential to the East German official. It was almost like he was begging for enough jet fuel to get us back to the U.S. When permission was finally granted, the pilot was obsequious in his thanks. All of the aircrew on board seemed much relieved. I had the impression that the Poles had pulled this stunt so many times that the East Germans were running out of patience with them…

But our luck was holding. We were re-fueled, back in the air and headed home. JKF never looked so good as we arrived late in the day. I felt like running out on the runway and kissing the ground…The customs agent welcomed me home and I had a very emotional reaction, which surprised me. As tired as I was, I never felt better in my life. I transferred to a domestic flight and arrived back in Seattle late that evening. With the 10 hour time difference, it had been a very long day.

The next morning was Saturday and my family and friends were all interested in my trip. For a short while, I was the center of attention. My fame did not last that long, however, and by the next day, Sunday May 18th, 1980 I was totally upstaged by the eruption of Mount St. Helens. It provided a final exclamation point to my Polish adventure and embedded it in my memory forever.

But there were a few interesting postscripts to the trip; it was several months later that I found out about Dick, the software engineer who accompanied me on the trip. I was shocked and saddened to find out that, the week after I left, Dick's wife had suddenly passed away in Phoenix. But Dick was prepared...He had executed our "escape plan", traveling to Gdansk and then by ferry across the Baltic to Sweden, where he was able to purchase airline tickets back to Phoenix.

Years went by. It was now 1995 and my wife and I had moved to California so that I could take over a resident Honeywell contract, writing control software and supporting our new, Total Distributed Control Computer System at U.S.S. Posco, a joint-venture steel mill in the Bay Area. I wanted my wife, Sheila, to see some of the countries that I had visited with Honeywell back in the early days, so we scheduled a three week tour with Trafalgar. The trip started in England. After several days of sightseeing we traveled to Harwich and boarded an overnight ferry for Denmark. From Denmark we traveled to Sweden and then took another overnight ferry to Finland. "Remember now", our tour guide told us as we were about to enter Russia, "this is an adventure, not a vacation". She was certainly right about that. Two years earlier the Soviet Union had collapsed and Russia was in the midst of chaos. From Finland we traveled by bus to St. Petersburg and then to Moscow. From there we traveled through Belarus to Warsaw, where we spent the night.

I could not believe the transformation from Communism to Capitalism. Colorful awnings covered the buildings in Warsaw. Kentucky Fried

Chicken, McDonalds and other joint-venture companies advertised their wares prominently. People were well dressed and the streets were filled with expensive European cars. No military personnel were in sight. And the Palace of Culture? Stalin's Wedding Cake? Stalin's present to the People of Poland? The building was closed and scheduled for demolition... I was so proud of the Polish people...

WPPSS

Big Government... How could this be happening to us? It was one of the worst disasters ever to occur in the State of Washington since the last glacial age, when the ice dam melted, creating the Columbia River. It all began with Bonneville Power Administration, then a part of the Department of the Interior. The experience they had obtained building hydroelectric dams on the Columbia during the Depression and for years thereafter, had given them a false confidence in the infallibility of their logic. Unfortunately, it is the nature of government to grow, so it was no great surprise that by the nineteen seventies, BPA had decided that by the year 2000, Washington State would be totally out of power and would require massive new generation facilities. Unfortunately, that assumption was totally false.

But life was good for us back then. We had the cheapest electricity in the world, with hydroelectric dams on the Columbia at Bonneville, John Day, The Dalles, McNary, Chief Joe, Wanapum, Priest Rapids, Rocky Reach and the granddaddy of them all, Grand Coulee. Honeywell had 4020 computer systems at the D.C. converter station at Celillo Falls and The Dalles dam, and dual 4010 systems at the BPA Control Center in Vancouver, to which a number of the dams were connected by microwave link. If more or less electrical generation was required from the dams, the Control Center would send out a "raise" or "lower" signal from its computer by microwave. The signal would be received at dams up the Columbia and their computer systems would incrementally open or close the giant gates that controlled the flow of water through the turbines, altering the amount of generation. The system worked so flawlessly and so cheaply, that only a minimum number of operators were in attendance anywhere in the system.

And there were many other dams, including those on the Snake River and even smaller hydro units on some of the irrigation canals in Eastern Washington. We had plenty of power, so much so that providers were given awards for maintaining electrical costs to customers at ONE CENT PER KILOWATT HOUR. Home builders in those years were given huge incentives to build "ALL ELECTRIC HOMES" in order to sell the power that was being developed. These were good times...

We had so much power, in fact, that it was decided to build a "D.C. Link" in order to supply the excess generation to Southern California, an area, which, as usual, was desperate. This was no mean feat. Because of the energy losses in a 1000 mile long alternating current (A.C.) power line, it was decided to build a converter station to jack up the A.C. voltage and then to convert it to Direct Current (D.C.) at 500,000 volts. Beginning at the Celilo Falls converter station on the Columbia, the D.C. line stretched southward to the Los Angeles area, ending at the Sylmar Converter Station, where the D.C. voltage would be converted back to A.C. for normal consumption. The amazing thing is that the project actually worked. There was just one small problem...In the dry season, grass fires burning in the mountains filled the air with smoke particles. These particles became a "conductive path" for the 500,000 volt D.C. line. From its high tension towers, the D.C. line would suddenly short to ground, popping all the circuit breakers. Because of the extraordinarily high voltage, sometimes the line would "go out" for no reason at all, or at least no reason that could be understood. It was suspected that, under certain conditions, the voltage was high enough to "ionize" the air and cause a spontaneous discharge...Almost like lightning...Spooky...

But what was stranger still was that Friday morning that I got a call from the Celilo Converter Station. The D.C. line was up but the 4020 computer system was reporting a problem with the digital subsystem, which sent and received commands to operate the station. I talked at length by phone to the technician on site, who was convinced that the problem was a digital output problem. I gave him some suggestions for troubleshooting the system. At the end of the conversation, I told him that I could throw some clothes in a bag, grab my tools, and drive down to the site, but it was already midday on a Friday and it would take me at least five hours to get there. Our contract only covered weekday hours, so, after some discussion, he decided to work on the problem himself until I could get there on Monday.

I thought nothing more about it the rest of that day. The next day I went about my regular routine, mowing the lawn and generally relaxing. It was not until Saturday night when I turned on the news that I was to go into a state of shock…The announcer was explaining something about a huge power outage in San Francisco. The cable cars had stopped dead in their tracks, homes and businesses were without power, and traffic lights were out. The outage lasted over six hours. The whole outage was somehow being blamed on the "D.C. Intertie" as the transmission line was known. "Uh oh", I thought to myself, "I think I know where this is going".

I was fit to be tied. I thought about it all day Sunday…I read the Sunday papers. The only information that I could get was that the D.C. line had gone down, causing power transmission from Washington to California to shift over to the A.C. lines. The A.C. transmission lines were already running at peak load to supply air conditioning needs in Southern California, so they could not handle any more power. It was a disaster. The A.C. lines had overloaded and gone down. The generators on the Columbia River dams were now disconnected from their load in California, so they went into overspeed and tripped out. The whole grid was down. It was a nightmare. Was it caused by something I told the technician to do? I thought about it…a lot…

I couldn't wait to get into my car the next morning. It was a long drive; the closer I got to the site, the more nervous I became. Was this going to be my fault? Was there going to be a lawsuit? I arrived at the Converter Station and walked in, not knowing what to expect. I was totally shocked. Everything was normal. People were walking about as usual. They greeted me pleasantly. It was Big Government. It was no one's fault. There appeared to be no individual responsibility assigned, as far as I could determine. The station was up, the D.C. line was up; all was well with the world. I was much relieved.

I walked back into the computer room. The computer was running, but it was still printing out error reports referencing the digital input/output system. I greeted the technician. And then the whole story came out.

After our telephone conversation on Friday, the technician continued to work on the problem without success. He came back to the site on Saturday morning, determined to find a solution. He told operators to take the system off computer control so that he could shut down the computer and load an offline diagnostic program. He had discovered a small switch on the side of the digital system cabinet, a part of the computer system, labeled "Test" and "Normal", so he assumed that in the "Test" mode, he would be protected from actually putting out digital signals that controlled the station. He was dead wrong. For those of us working in the Honeywell world of computers, it was axiomatic that to "assume" something, meant to "make an <u>ass</u> of <u>u</u> and <u>me.</u>

And so it was that the technician loaded the digital output diagnostic program. The program was only meant to be used in a factory setting and without any "real world" connections attached to the digital outputs. When the test switch was set to "test", a single output was "looped back" to a single input so the output operation could be verified. Otherwise, the diagnostic program triggered every single output in the cabinet. Unfortunately, one of the outputs was connected to a "shut down" relay for the entire Converter Station. And thus it was that on the Saturday morning in question, the entire Converter Station had gone offline, triggering a massive failure.

I approached the computer with trepidation. Would I be the second person in as many days to shut down the grid? I told the operators to take the system off computer control. And then I shut down the computer. I analyzed the error print outs and then I loaded a small machine language diagnostic program. I took out my scope, extended a circuit board, and looked at a few points. The problem, I discovered finally, was not in the digital output system but in the digital input system. I changed out one of the digital input circuit boards and loaded the operating system back up on the computer. The computer came up, checked out the digital input/output system and was satisfied. It reported no more errors. I told the operators to put the Converter Station back in computer control. Everyone breathed a sigh of relief.

I wrote a report, shook hands with the technician and left the site. It was late in the day and it was a long drive home. I proceeded East, up the Columbia Gorge, a remote and beautiful part of Washington and Oregon, with the Cascade Mountains rising up thousands of feet on either side of the river. The sun was setting, casting long shadows across the roadway. It was breathtakingly beautiful, but I needed to find a motel. I drove and drove. Finally, around a bend in the river I came to a small town. It was Biggs, Oregon. It should have been called "Smalls, Oregon" because there was only one restaurant and two motels. Unfortunately, when the Greyhound Bus came to town, late in the afternoon, the population of the town doubled and no rooms were available. Finally, I told the desk clerk, "Are you sure you don't have any rooms?" "Well", he told me, I am totally full. The only thing I have left is the Executive Suite. It has two bedrooms, two air conditioners, two TV sets and a living room". "Fine", I said, "I'll take it". He looked at me with concern. He was embarrassed about telling me the price of the suite. "I don't know", he said, shaking his head, "It's eighteen dollars a night!" I accepted on the spot. I turned on both air conditioners and both TV sets. It was wonderful.

Half an hour later I walked out of my air conditioned paradise and over to a local diner. I grabbed a hamburger and read the local paper. There were no movie theaters in Biggs, but in The Dalles, where I had just been, there was a theater playing "Shampoo" with Warren Beatty. There was a late showing so I got into the car and retraced my route back down the Gorge.

I found the theater, purchased my ticket and went in. There were only a few people in the theater, which I thought was not unusual for a Monday night. The show started and I got involved in the plot, which was fairly light, but entertaining. Suddenly, half way through the film the projector stopped and the lights went on. I couldn't believe it. I asked the manager, "What's going on?" "What do you mean", he said..."The film stopped", I said. "Oh", he said, "It's the rule.". "The Rule?" I asked, incredulously..."Yes", he told me, "when there are less than 12 people in the theater, we shut down the film." "Oh", I said... Apparently the twelfth person had just left the theater...All the way back to Biggs I wondered how the plot turned out...In fact, I still do...And then I wondered why "The Rule" was 12-based instead of 10-based...Working with computers and digital numbering systems had endlessly complicated my life...

I drove back to Seattle and my life returned to normal. But, as I was soon to discover, my experience dealing with the Converter Station disaster was small potatoes compared to what was to become a boondoggle so bad that it would be called "the worst municipal bond default in U.S. history". In its infinite wisdom, the Bonneville Power Administration had convinced the local utilities that a huge "power shortage" was about to occur in the year 2000 based upon their assumptions that power demand would double every 10 years. To deal with this issue the utilities had bonded together, under legislative approval, to form a public-private agency known as the Washington Public Power Supply System, or WPPSS. The acronym was pronounced "Whoops", which was to become emblematic of the apocalypse about to occur.

But I get ahead of myself…The government's first impetus was to add more hydroelectric dams, something that it had done so well since the nineteen thirties. Unfortunately, there was only one "damable" spot left on the Columbia, at Hanford Reach. Putting a dam here would only add a minimal amount to the overall generation capacity, so a new solution would be required. And it was here that the government agencies involved extended themselves out of their comfort zone. To solve the imaginary "power shortage" problem, WPPSS would build FIVE NUCLEAR PLANTS…Plant Two would be the first plant built at the Hanford Nuclear Reservation in Eastern Washington, the facility that produced one of the atomic bombs in WWII. Plants 1 and 4 would be also built at Hanford, while Plants 3 and 5 would be built at Satsop in Western Washington, not far from the coast.

This was a total mis-calculation. No one had ever built a nuclear plant before nor had ever supervised the construction of one. Contractors were selected who were totally incompetent and had no construction experience in projects of this dimension. Cost overruns were common. To quote from HistoryLink.org,

"Several factors combined to ruin construction schedules and to drive costs to three and four times the original estimates. Inflation and design changes constantly plagued all the projects. Builders often got ahead of designers who modified their drawings to conform to what had been built. Safety changes imposed by the Nuclear Regulatory Commission increased costs too, but the biggest cause of delays and overruns was mismanagement of the process by the WPPSS. The directors and the managers of the system had no experience in nuclear engineering or in projects of this scale. System managers were unable to develop a unified and comprehensive means of choosing, directing, and supervising contractors. One contractor, already shown to be incompetent, was retained for more work. In a well-publicized example, a pipe hanger was built and rebuilt 17 times. Quality control inspectors complained of inadequate work that went unaddressed."

I read stories in the paper of workmen who had reportedly dropped wheel barrows into the pouring of the containment vessel, a thick concrete shell housing the reactor core, compromising its integrity and causing total rework. I read of costly vacations taken by employees, all "on the taxpayer dime". Every time the public complained about excessive costs, WPPSS would explain that they would pay the costs from the profits of reactors online. They only problem was; they never got any reactors on line…That is, with the exception of one, the Number Two plant at Hanford. I installed the 4010 computer system there and upgraded the memory, along with a team of wire wrappers from Phoenix and another field engineer.

The next plant to be completed was the Number Three Plant at Satsop. It was 1980, the plant was 80% complete and I was in Phoenix familiarizing myself with the computer system, which was in "staging" at the Honeywell Peoria plant. I had received reams of system documents for the installation and was preparing to install the 4500 Computer System at the site sometime in early summer. It never happened. WPPSS went bankrupt early in the year, defaulting on 2.25 Billion dollars of municipal bonds, the largest recorded default in U.S. history. All construction was shut down at Hanford 1 and 4 and Satsop 3 and 5. Construction was never resumed and the plants were eventually scheduled for destruction. The price of electricity to the consumer jumped from one cent a kilowatt hour to 15 cents per kilowatt hour. So much for cheap electrical power in the Northwest…

But I was wrong…WPPSS Plant 3 at Satsop WAS capable of generating revenue…Just not in the way that I thought. Years later I took my father on a "Plant Tour" of the shuttered nuclear plant. There was the Honeywell 4500 computer system that I had been scheduled to install, cabinets painted in Caribbean blue, sitting in pristine elegance in the middle of the control room. I took out my Honeywell keys and opened a cabinet door. Everything was in place. Then I paid the admittance fee to the tour director…

Puerto la Cruz

I don't know how I kept getting involved with these things. One of the reasons, I suspected, was that our Field Engineering Services group was understaffed. With the purchase of General Electric's Process Computer Division, it had been necessary for Honeywell had to create its own service group, which now numbered about 30 people. Each of us had to cover our own area, and, in addition, be able to fly anywhere in the world should there be a need. This often caused problems when a computer specialist left his area and a problem arose.

But this was not really a "short handed" issue; this was an issue with ME. I was all too available. Living in the Seattle area in the early 'eighties, I found that my contract responsibilities were relatively light, which made me a target. I had customers at Olympic Pipeline in Renton, Burlington Northern Railroad in Pasco, and Bonneville Power in Vancouver, but each of these sites had their own computer maintenance personnel, and so unless there was a serious problem, I made only routine visits.

And then one day I received a call from Phoenix asking me if I could go to Venezuela. I could not get a clear definition of the problems the customer was having, but, having nothing better to do, I agreed. Traveling through Venezuela, as it turned out, was not a simple problem. It was easy enough to get a flight to Caracas, connecting through Miami, but it was another story getting to the job site, traveling from one point to another, or escaping from the grasp of the Venezuelan government…

And so it was that one spring morning in 1981 I boarded a flight bound for Caracas. With the usual delays and the time difference, it was early evening before I arrived. I walked out of the airport looking for a cab. I surveyed the fleet of taxis pulled up to the curb. They all looked like "gypsy" drivers to me. I did not see any of the "radio cabs" with lights on the top, so I picked one at random and gave him my hotel address. That was a huge mistake…The driver was so eager to get a fare and a huge tip that he tore off at full speed, passing other drivers on the shoulder of the road. He grinned back at me for approval as he sped at breakneck speed along the freeways outside the city. I was terrified. I couldn't wait to get to the hotel, which was in the downtown area. Finally, we arrived. I tipped the driver and checked in.

I went to the hotel bar and had a cerveza, in fact I had several cervezas. After dinner I decided to take a walk. I had noticed, from the air, a whole city of shacks on the outskirts of town. These were the under-class, as I was to discover. In the city, I passed by the houses of the upper class, who lived in villas with broken glass embedded on the tops of the surrounding walls and guard dogs inside the gates. It was definitely a two-class society. I looked in the shop windows. Shirts were displayed at a price of forty U.S. dollars which, in 1981, was ridiculously high.

At the end of the block was an automobile dealership, displaying expensive European cars. The display was well lit and in an open air setting, so I stepped in to admire them. I could not understand how, in this society, these cars could be displayed without protection. I soon found out. As I approached the cars, a guard suddenly appeared. This did not look like a good opportunity for a confrontation, so I retreated back to the sidewalk and returned to my hotel.

The next morning, I took a cab to the Honeywell offices in Caracas and met the branch manager and a salesman. It was necessary to fill out an enormous amount of paperwork just to work in Venezuela. The Venezuelan government insisted than anyone working in the country, even for a few weeks, should pay an income tax equal to 20% of any income received. Honeywell planned to pay this tax for me, so we discussed "adjusting" my reported salary to minimize the extortion. Before our discussions were concluded, however, the Honeywell salesman took an emergency telephone call. Suddenly, he departed. There was a problem with his new house…

When I asked about the emergency, the manager explained to me that, in Venezuela, the water supply was always a problem, so homes were built with a large cistern in the basement. In the rainy season, water from the roof was directed into the cistern, where it was stored so that it could be pumped up during the dry part of the year. In this case, the salesman's cistern had developed a leak. The water was flowing out and threatening to wash away the foundation. I couldn't imagine this happening anywhere in the States…

Finally, my office paperwork was completed and I headed to the airport for my short flight to Barcelona, the nearest town to my final destination. Once reaching Barcelona, the plan was for me to rent a car and drive the remaining distance to Puerto la Cruz. I stood in line at the car rental company for what seemed an interminable length of time. Finally, it was my turn. Car theft was a serious problem in Venezuela, so the available rentals were really downscale. I ended up with a yellow Ford that had seen its better days. The car would not start. The keys that I had been given were on an unusually long chain. When I examined the chain, I discovered a second key. I searched around and found that the rental company had installed a second ignition lock under the dash to thwart thievery. Finally, with both ignition keys installed, the car started and I proceeded on my way, with the long chain rattling against the dashboard.

Driving in Venezuela was treacherous. No one seemed to stop at stop signs and roads were extremely narrow and confusing. I had to guess at a lot of intersections. My blood pressure was through the roof. Finally, after about an hour of driving, I arrived in Puerto la Cruz and found my hotel. I was really impressed. This was a resort hotel on the shores of the Caribbean. My room had a small balcony looking out upon the ocean and the small beach where guests sunbathed and waded in the surf. On the horizon I could see cruise ships headed towards Isle de la Margarita, a popular resort destination. I felt much better already.

But now, back to work. I gathered my toolbox and headed down to the parking lot. My next assignment was to find Vencemos, a cement plant several miles away. There was only one road that followed the ocean in that direction, so I began to relax. WHOA! Rounding a curve I was stopped dead in my tracks by a checkpoint. When I rolled down my window, a Venezuelan soldier shoved a machine gun in my face, with his finger on the trigger. I had no idea what was going on. I showed them my passport. I was sure they could not read English, but I was equally sure they could "blow me away" in a heartbeat if I resisted.

That really got my heart pumping. What the heck was going on? It took me a while to piece together the entire picture. To begin with, as I was find out, there were only two countries in the entire continent of South America that had civilian governments, which meant that they were the only ones not ruled by military dictatorship. Those countries were Brazil and Venezuela. Because their market economies worked, they were also the wealthiest countries in South America. The vast amount of offshore oil in Venezuelan also helped in that regard. Despite the success of their free market economy, however, Venezuela was rapidly turning into a Socialist state, which explained why their Bolivar was only worth .005 U.S. dollars. All industries had been nationalized, including the Shell refinery and other American refineries on the "ABC" islands of Aruba, Bonaire, and Curacao just off the coast. All nationalized industries had been renamed with "ven" in their titles, indicating their government status. Vencemos, Paraven, and Maraven were just some of the examples.

But what did that have to do with the military checkpoints? Because of the wealth in Venezuela, the country had become a target for some of the other desperately poor nations, such as Columbia, which was its next door neighbor. Columbians, in an effort to escape from dire poverty were literally invading Venezuela, coming over the border as illegal aliens and threatening to destroy the country's economy. The Venezuelan government responded by installing checkpoints at intervals along its roadways to detect and deport Columbians and other aliens who sought to enter the country illegally. It was a chilling experience…

Finally, after much discussion between the soldiers, my passport was returned and I was waved onwards. Luckily, the cement plant was in site. I turned into the parking lot, grabbed my tool box and entered the building. I located the plant engineer, who conducted me on a brief tour through the cement plant. The high point of the tour was the mainframe 4010 Honeywell computer system, installed in the center of the building. There was only one problem…All the lights on the front panel were out. Apparently, it had not been running for a very long time…

"Uh-oh", I thought to myself…"This is going to be a problem". Computer systems in those early days were composed of many individual, small integrated circuits and transistors, all of which were installed on circuit boards plugged into a massive backpanel. The whole system was extremely sensitive to temperature and humidity. Experienced service people knew that if a computer system ran for years and it became necessary to shut it down, it might not come back. Circuits that had been performing marginally, when cooled down, would fail on start up. One of the people in our group was so paranoid about the situation that, at a company in Oklahoma, he had remained on site for an entire week during the yearly plant shutdown in order to keep the computer running, opening up its doors and cabinets and cooling the circuits with box fans.

This was not the case at Vencemos. As I opened the door of the first cabinet, the first thing I was saw was a coating of rust on its steel surfaces. I couldn't believe it. Obviously the air conditioning in the room had failed some time ago, leaving the computer exposed to the heat and humidity of the Caribbean climate. This was not going to be easy. I turned on the power switch…Nothing happened.

This was the beginning of a massive effort to restore the computer to operation. I worked as long as I could that day, going back to the hotel only after I was too tired to think any more. It was late when I arrive back in Puerto la Cruz, and the restaurant was closed, so I ate in the bar, which offered a cheaper and simpler menu. This was to become a daily ritual as I fought my way through problems back at the plant.

I awoke the next morning with sunlight streaming through the sliding glass door. I walked out onto the balcony looked out over the intense blue of the sea. Honeywell had decided to paint all of their computer cabinets Caribbean Blue; now I could appreciate the choice. I could see the white hulls of vessels in the distance and guests lounging on the beach. "If only I were on vacation", I thought to myself. I walked into the bathroom and flipped on the light switch. Nothing happened.

I stood there for a moment. There was sufficient light coming through the door to attempt a shave, so I walked over to the sink and turned on the tap. Nothing came out. Then I remembered some sage advice from an old traveler that I had met…I walked over to the toilet and scooped some water from the bowl. I had enough water to shave and do a quick face wash. I thought about brushing my teeth, but immediately decided against it. As I knew from my previous experience in Caracas, water was scarce in Venezuela and often had to be pumped from cisterns in the basement, where it was collected in the rainy season. When the power went out, so did the pumps. I dressed and went downstairs.

The breakfast was served, as I was to discover, out of doors in a lush tropical setting. I complained about the loss of power but no one seemed the least concerned. I was frustrated. Especially frustrating were the tiny cups of coffee that were served for breakfast. I located the coffee urn and found some larger, American style cups, which I filled to the brim. I sat down and looked out over the sea. The breeze was warm and soothing. I relaxed…but only for a few moments…Slowly I began to discover the rationale behind the tiny cups…The coffee had a good strong flavor but was also full of caffeine. I could feel my blood pressure rising and my ears ringing…I would stick to the small cups from now on…

I drove back to the plant. When I fixed one problem, I would discover another. To get one subsystem to work, I would have to fix another subsystem. And on and on it went. The spare parts on the site were minimal; I quickly exhausted the supply of circuit boards. Now I would have to use my Tektronix scope to troubleshoot problems down to the component level. I had to devise machine language programs and load them on the computer, forcing certain functions to repetitively "loop" so I could scope the signals and isolate the problem.

I repaired boards, one after another, but I was running out of computer chips from the customer's supply. Luckily, I had a small supply of my own chips in my tool box. Finally, most of the system was ready to be tested on line. I loaded the operating system from the rotating drum memory… It died…I had no clue…I decided to load and run the AU or arithmetic unit diagnostic test, which analyzed the basic functionality of the machine. The test failed. I couldn't believe it…I had fixed all the other problems that I could find…I did some more investigation and discovered that the test had failed on the DIVIDE function.

I was appalled. Of all the instructions that the computer executed, the DIVIDE was the absolutely most complex of all, involving something like 17 steps, known as "sequence states". I spent the next 12 hours "stepping" the machine through each of the steps, trying to find the problem. Eventually, I isolated a failed signal, which I traced to a bad chip. In the world of digital logic, signals were either a "one", at 4 to 5 volts, or a "zero" of 0.5 to 1.5 volts. Any signal in the 2 to 3 volt range could not be interpreted in the machine as a "one" or "zero", causing the logic to fail.

I replaced the bad chip and re-ran the diagnostic test. Success! The diagnostic test ran to completion with no errors found. At last, I could load the operating system…or not. I loaded the operating system from drum memory and the printer responded…I was running! …but wait….there was still a problem with the digital output system that was causing the operating system to fail to completely initialize.

Time was running short…I had extended my work hours to try to make my deadline. On my final day, I made the decision to work 24 hours straight in a last ditch effort. The long hours and the mental strain were getting to me. I began to feel a throat infection coming on. I absolutely could not succumb. By sheer act of will I refused to get sick. I worked all night trying to solve the final problems. At about 3:00 a.m., I ran totally out of spare chips…There was only one solution left…Get some more chips and circuit boards and return to the site.

I was very concerned that, even if the computer were restored to operation, it could not function long without some on-site support. I made a long list of circuit boards and chips that the customer needed to purchase and then I told him that he needed to hire a competent computer professional to maintain the system. I was not sure that I was communicating well with the plant manager, but I did convince him that someone from Honeywell would be returning to the site to finish the last repairs.

I was exhausted. I returned to the hotel and checked out. On the first day I had managed to drop my room key in the parking lot and had driven off without it. Someone had used it to enter my room and attempted to open my suitcase, which was locked. I noticed that the latches had been turned but that the lock had prevented the suitcase from opening. My travel money was safe inside, so there was not a problem. When I asked for a new key at the desk, they told me they would have to manufacture one, so they gave me a master room key to use. I couldn't believe it…what kind of security was that? Finally, on the last day of my stay, I got a proper room key…

I was dog tired, I drove to the airport at Barcelona. I almost crashed on the roadway trying to avoid another car….I was not sure of the route, but, finally, I recognized some of the buildings that I had passed on the way in. The airport was in sight, at last and I turned in my car with a great sense of relief. But nothing was that simple…The rental car manager insisted on inspecting every inch of my car to find out if there was any way that he could charge me for a repair. He found nothing…I was greatly encouraged. I waded into the check-in line at the counter. These people were pushing and shoving. They did not allow the person-to-person space that I was accustomed to. If a left a space between myself and the person in front of me, someone would "cut in". Finally, I got to the counter and checked in my bag. The flight back to Caracas was peaceful and uneventful.

I had been directed to report back to the Honeywell office in Caracas before I departed for the U.S. I did not understand why I couldn't just fly back to the States. "Because", they told me, "You need your Solvencia". They explained in great detail that I had to have a document that proved the payment of my income tax to the Venezuelan government. I couldn't believe it. It was already getting late in the day and the government offices would soon be closing. The Honeywell office had sent a runner to obtain the document, but it was going to be a toss up whether he could make it in time. I had an early morning flight the next day, but without the Solvencia, I would not be allowed to board. Finally, the runner appeared with the document in hand. I thanked him and headed to my hotel for a good night's sleep.

I was beginning to get a little paranoid about government intrusion in my life…What other hurdles might I face boarding my flight? I decided to take no chances, so I arranged for a 5:00 a.m. taxi to the airport for an 8:30 departure. It was still dark as I entered the airport.

I immediately headed for the Pan Am desk, which was open. I tried to check in my bag, but there was a problem. I could not understand the language. How could checking in my bag be a problem? I showed them all of my documentation, but they kept waving their hands: "No, No!". Finally, an English speaking clerk explained, "Señor, you must pay your baggage tax!" I still had some Bolivars left so I paid the tax. They accepted my bag, finally and issued me a boarding pass. Thank goodness…Now I was good to go…

I approached the entrance to the international boarding area. I showed the guard my passport. He shook his head vigorously. "No, No", he said. Then I showed him my Solvencia and my baggage tax receipt. No luck…He kept waving his arms back towards the main part of the terminal. Finally I turned around and saw a kiosk in the center of the floor. Reluctantly, I approached the kiosk. The sign above the window, in Spanish, read, as best as I could determine, something like "Airport Tax". Not a problem, I thought to myself…I still had a few Bolivars, so I complied. I received my Airport Tax receipt and headed back to the boarding area. I showed the guard every document I had.. My passport, my Solvencia, my baggage tax receipt and my airport tax receipt. "No, No", he kept repeating, waving his arms back towards the kiosk that I had just recently visited. I tried to explain to him that I had already been to that window, but he wouldn't listen. Finally, in desperation, I looked back, one more time at the kiosk. It was only then that I began to realize that the kiosk was actually "double sided". Slowly, I plodded back towards the kiosk and walked around to the opposite side. There, in bold letters, above the windows were the words "Departure Tax". I couldn't believe it. I paid the tax with the last Bolivars I had left and headed back to the boarding area. This time, the guard let me through into the international departure lounge. I was free at last…Goodbye Socialism, hello Democracy….I sat down in a chair and watched the sun come up…It was going to be a good day.

Months passed. I heard nothing from the Venezuelans. Finally, one morning about a year later I got a call to return to the Vencemos site.

The problem appeared to be communication errors with the drum memory, which surprised me. Apparently the system was running. This time I knew the drill and my transit through the Venezuelan system proceeded without a hitch. I arrived on site and was introduced to the new system maintenance person, and ex-IBM field engineer who was highly qualified. He toured me through the system. The computer was running, the air conditioning was functioning, and a huge parts inventory had been purchased. I was stunned.

The new field engineer was quite friendly. He spoke English well and had been thoroughly trained at the Honeywell School in Phoenix. Together we worked through the system problems, which were minimal. Several days later, as I was preparing to depart, I had to ask him a question. I knew that the cement plant had spent a bundle of money getting this system back in operation. "In our country", I explained, "we look at something we call the cost/benefit ratio. In other words, the cost of investment must be balanced by an increase in productivity." "So, I said, you must really be getting some financial benefit from this system".

He stared at me. Moments passed…"I do not think you understand", he said slowly, parsing his words. "In Venezuela, things are different." I was puzzled. "What do you mean?", I asked him. And then the truth came out. "THIS COMPUTER IS JUST FOR SHOW", he explained. "We bring customers through the plant. We show them the computer. They are very impressed". I was in a state of shock.

Then he took me into the plant area that was controlled by the computer. He was absolutely right. Every computer-controlled area had a station with a selection switch. There was a "computer control" position on the switch and a "manual control" position. Every switch was in the "manual control" position. I couldn't believe it. My whole death-defying effort had been "just for show"…"My God", I thought to myself, "This is a SOCIALIST PARADISE!"

I flew back to Seattle business class, as had been permitted by General

Electric for overseas travel. Next to me was a wealthy businessman who tried to interest me in his daughter on my next trip to Venezuela. He invited me to his villa in Caracas and I accepted, knowing that there was no way I was going to return. Women in South America were always interested in "hooking up" with Americans, so I gave it little thought.

Life resumed again for me in Seattle. Normally, I just worked out of my house, but this day in particular I went into the Honeywell office on Mercer Island. I ran into Van, whom I had worked with previously on a State of Washington contract. "Hey", he said, "Thanks for sending me that postcard from Venezuela". I was surprised. "You're welcome", I replied. Walking out to the car I hesitated. Something wasn't quite right…Then I remembered…The postcard I had sent Van was from my trip to Venezuela a year ago…He had just gotten it in the mail…

Cofrentes

General Electric needed assistance. The company was in the process of installing a nuclear Boiling Water Reactor in Cofrentes, Spain. Unfortunately, the process of building a nuclear plant customarily takes about ten years, so the Spanish company, Hidroelectrica Espanola, had purchased the Honeywell computer system in the early phases of the project, sometime in 1975. It was now 1983, and the majority of the system had been in storage on site for at least eight years. The exception was the processor itself, a Honeywell 4010, which had been installed in one of the office spaces and was now running.

During the eight or so years since the system was delivered, the software requirements had grown significantly, so there was a need to expand the memory and to add other features and devices, all of which required weeks of installation time. When complete, the upgraded 4010 processor was to be installed in the reactor computer room along with all of the numerous digital and analog input and output cabinets and a video system, all of which had been sitting in warehouses since day one. There was also a custom data acquisition system designed by GE using Honeywell hardware that had to be added. To upgrade everything, bring it together, and make it play was a major assignment.

And so it was that the General Electric manager on the Cofrentes site contacted the local Honeywell office in Spain. Unfortunately, because of the age of the computer, Honeywell España could not supply anyone with the proper knowledge or experience, so GE then called Honeywell in Phoenix. But Honeywell in Phoenix could not directly send an engineer either, and for very good reasons.

The problem was that a bureaucratic re-organization had taken place in 1980, when our computer services group, all thirty of us, had been called to Denver for a special meeting. We were staying at a fancy hotel and being treated, in the evening, to an expensive "wild game dinner". Unfortunately, I had taken an evening flight from Seattle which, with delays, put me into town at about 3:00 a.m. Morning came early for me, so after a few hours sleep I went down to the meeting room.

And there the big plans were being laid out. At that time there were two industrial service groups: my old one, the analog instrumentation services group based in Fort Washington, Pa, and the new one, the computer services group, based in Phoenix. But technology was changing. The Fort Washington group had developed its own, smaller scale computer system known as the TDC 2000. It was now being integrated into our larger computer systems as a joint product. And it was creating a problem. Customers who purchased these systems would have to subscribe to two separate service organizations, which was not acceptable.

But that was not going to be an issue, according to our management. We would just take all of the TDC 2000 trained specialists into our group and assume their contracts. We were excited about the prospects of new technology and our management was excited about the new revenue. We all enjoyed our expensive wild game dinner and returned home.

And then, two weeks later, I got the call. A second business meeting in Denver was being scheduled. I couldn't believe it. But this would be no wild game dinner or fancy hotel. We would be staying at a low budget motel and be on our own for meals. We would meet individually with our managers who would explain to us what had happened. We had been had...The larger instrumentation group, my old service organization, had gone to Honeywell management and convinced them to take all of the computer people into their group. I was stunned...I would be returning to my old instrumentation group after having escaped into the computer world for five years...There was going to be a major cultural conflict...

And so it was that the request for assistance from GE would have to travel all the way down the management chain of the new service organization to Bill, my new manager in Mercer Island, Washington. Bill then contacted me, asking if I wanted to go to Spain. I had worked for Bill back in Union, New Jersey, in the analog instrumentation days after I first started with Honeywell, so I knew him well. He was an honest and straightforward manager, so much so that his management had presented him with a "straight arrow" which he proudly taped to his office door. Incredibly, he still allowed me to work out of my house, although he could have required that I report to the office every day. I respected him for that.

And there was another huge benefit that Bill and the new group provided. I had been shifted from a classification of "salaried, exempt" to "salaried, non-exempt" which meant that, from now on, all those lengthy hours of work on computer systems would be compensated with overtime pay. I was very pleased with that situation. However, there was definitely a conflict that existed with my new organization. I had worked out of my house previously as an independent agent, scheduling my own flights with an Air Travel Card and paying my expenses by company Traveletter. In my new organization, freedom was severely limited, people were required to report to the office, and management made all decisions. And so it was the Bill decided to "help me" by making reservations for me to go to Spain.

He couldn't have picked worse flights. He was so proud of himself as he showed me the itinerary: a United flight from Seattle to JFK, an SAS flight from JFK to Copenhagen, and an SAS flight from Copenhagen to Valencia, Spain. ARRRGGH! But it was even worse on the return… The SAS flight from Valencia back to Copenhagen could not connect with the return flight to JFK, so it was necessary to spend an extra night at the SAS Hotel in Copenhagen. "You surely don't mind spending the night in Copenhagen?" he asked, looking at me for approval…I couldn't have been more appalled. The last thing I wanted to do was spend one more night in a foreign hotel. But I kept a brave face, thinking to myself that I would change the reservations with my Air Travel card as soon as I got a chance.

It was too late to change the outbound flight, so I reported to SeaTac airport as planned and boarded a United Boeing 747 for JFK. I looked out the window…dense fog. We taxied out and then stopped dead in our tracks. And we waited. Now I was beginning to worry…If any of these flights were delayed, the whole schedule would fall apart. There was only one overseas flight a night for each airline from JFK to European destinations, so if I missed it, I would lose an entire day. My thoughts were interrupted by the sound of the engines spinning down. The engine noise faded away and it became dead quiet… Then the air handling system shut down and slowly the passenger compartment began to cool….I could see nothing from my window except shades of gray…

The delay continued…I looked at my watch…Forty minutes had gone by. It was getting more and more difficult to make my SAS connection in New York. A click; the loudspeaker system turned on and the captain began his explanation; the visibility was below minimum for takeoff and two wide-bodied jets, one ahead of us and one behind us, were preventing us from moving in any direction. And that was the reason we were stopped dead on the taxiway with the engines off. The captain appeared to be worried that we might hold him personally responsible for the delay, so he sought to deflect the blame by inviting any passenger who was interested to come up to the cockpit and see for himself. I was sitting forward, and no one else was taking him up on his offer, so I walked up the aisle to the cockpit and stared out the windshield. I could just barely make out the tail of a DC-10 on the taxiway ahead of us in the fog. "Look", the captain said defensively, "you can barely see the tail of that aircraft and it's less than 100 feet away". I admitted that he was right, which, I think, made him feel a little less responsible, and walked back to my seat. What I didn't tell him was that in Seattle, in the month of December, this kind of fog could shut down the airport for days…

I went back to looking out the window. Suddenly, a brief patch of blue sky appeared above the fog. Seconds later I could hear the engines begin to wind up. The brakes unlocked with a jolt and we began to travel forward. Could we make it before the break in the fog disappeared? It was dicey… the fog bank was swirling in irregular patches, causing visibility to increase and then suddenly to decrease. I remembered the 1977 Tenerife crash when the fog caused two 747's to collide on the runway, killing over 500 people…We continued to taxi… I could hear the takeoff roar of one of the wide bodies ahead of us so I knew our turn was next… Finally we were at the end of the taxiway; I heard the brakes squeak as the aircraft turned to position itself on the main runway. We stopped. Clouds of fog blew by my window in slow motion…Minutes passed. Now we were cleared for takeoff…the aircraft shuddered as the engines went to full power…The brakes released suddenly and I could began to feel myself pushed into the seat back as we accelerated….Rotation and liftoff….I looked back as we cleared the runway. The hole in the fog was rapidly disappearing…we were lucky to get out at all….

We broke out into the clear air and sunshine and I looked down at the white blanket covering Puget Sound and Seattle. The fog filled the valleys and smaller hills but Mt. Rainier and the other Cascade volcanoes stood out in the bright sunshine, in amazing relief against the deep blue of the sky. It was going to be a good day…I relaxed in my seat and ordered breakfast.

The country unfolded beneath me. Five hours later, helped by a strong jet stream, we were on final approach to JFK. We landed on schedule and I walked over to the International Terminal. I checked the reader board. I had never flown SAS before, so I didn't quite know what to expect. I checked in at the gate and received my boarding pass. I stared out the window...CRAP! It was a McDonnell Douglas DC-10! I really hated DC-10's. My friend, Jim, a programmer was almost killed in 1979 when the flight that he usually took lost an engine on takeoff from Chicago O'Hare. Jim had been flying the Chicago-Los Angeles-Phoenix route on a weekly basis for months as he worked on an industrial project in the Chicago area. That particular week he had stayed in Phoenix, which saved his life.

The accident report stated: "Investigators found that as the jet was beginning its takeoff rotation, engine number one on the left (port) wing separated and flipped over the top of the wing. As the engine separated from the aircraft, it severed hydraulic fluid lines and damaged the left wing, resulting in a retraction of the slats. As the jet attempted to climb, the left wing aerodynamically stalled while the right wing, with its slats still deployed, continued to produce lift. The jetliner subsequently rolled to the left and reached a bank angle of 112 degrees (partially inverted), before impacting in an open field near a trailer park located near the end of the runway. The engine separation was attributed to damage to the pylon rigging structure holding the engine to the wing caused by inadequate maintenance procedures at American Airlines. All 258 passengers and 13 crew on board were killed, along with two persons on the ground. The accident remains the deadliest airliner accident to occur on United States soil, as well as the second deadliest involving a DC-10, after Turkish Airlines Flight 981".

And I was going to take this thing across the Atlantic Ocean? I didn't think it could fly that far! On one occasion, unfortunately, it couldn't... In 1998, an upgraded model, known as the MD11 and operated by SwissAir departed JFK in route to Switzerland. The aircraft caught fire and crashed into the Atlantic off the coast of Nova Scotia, killing All

229 people on board. It was the highest-ever death toll of any avia-tion accident involving a McDonnell Douglas MD-11. By the end of the Twentieth Century, the DC-10 and the upgraded MD11 had each managed to set all-time records for destroying people in air crashes. By 1998, all carriers except SwissAir had abandoned operation of the MD-11.

My thoughts returned to 1979, when, after the Chicago crash, the FAA grounded all DC-10's until it could be determined why the engine had fallen off. I had followed the news of the crash and the aftermath. Months went by and I continued to fly on other aircraft. I always liked the Seattle motto: "If it ain't Boeing, I ain't going!" But one fateful day I found myself returning from Phoenix to Seattle through Los Angeles. It wasn't until I was boarding at LAX that I discovered that I would be flying to Seattle on a DC-10. "I thought they were still grounded?" I asked the boarding agent. "Oh no!" she told me sweetly", "they were just released today". Lucky me. I sat grimly, staring out the window. I could hear the sound of the turbines winding up…The noise was exceptionally loud. It sounded like one of the engines might fall off at any minute…

But it wasn't just the engines falling off that bothered me, nor was it the fact that the aircraft was extremely noisy. There were other, little things; like the fact that the DC-10 had an abnormal habit of "blow-ing tires" on takeoff. One day, sitting on the ramp, I tried to figure out why. McDonnell Douglas DC-10's and Boeing 747's taxied by…I looked at the landing gear of both planes and slowly the reason became obvious…The 747's had approximately twice as many "tires on the ground" as the DC-10's. It appeared that the DC-10's were marginally-engineered in the landing gear department.

Finally we taxied out and departed. At full power, the engines sounded like they were straining, being pushed too hard…I could envision them ripping off at any minute… The mechanical noise level peaked to a high intensity, and for a second, I thought it was all over. Then the engines throttled back and I breathed a sigh of relief… I looked out the window…something was wrong already. Our normal departure from LAX took us out over the Pacific Ocean and up the coast to Washington. Today, we were over land, north of Los Angeles, and at a low altitude. I plugged in my headphones to the "pilot communication channel" which was provided for passengers. The channel monitored air to ground communication on takeoffs and landings and I always listened to the conversation.

There was some confusion…I could not exactly understand what was going on, but apparently the navigation system had selected the wrong beacon and the plane was proceeding on a course towards Pasadena. The ground controller was a little disturbed. After a brief, somewhat intense discussion, the controller corrected the flight crew. Seconds later, the plane banked sharply to the left and we flew out over the ocean, slowly turning to the north until we were headed towards Seattle. There was a "click" in my headphones and the communication channel abruptly disconnected…Too much information…

And so it was with some misgivings that I boarded the DC-10 SAS flight to Copenhagen in 1982. But the time passed smoothly and I relaxed, indulging myself in some alcoholic Danish beers which, when combined with the altitude, ended up giving me the headache of a lifetime. I had asked the beautiful Scandinavian flight attendant which beer she recommended, and she replied, "I don't drink beer", which made me feel even worse. We arrived in Copenhagen. I decided to go for a walk outside the terminal and get some fresh air. The smell of jet fuel almost made me gag, so I walked faster, as far away from the airport as I could get. The streets were very clean and empty of people. Everyone was at work…As I walked down the neat row of houses, I began to feel better. These were an industrious people who took great care of their houses and their city. I began to recover my positive attitude…

I walked back to the terminal. My next flight on SAS was on an Airbus, and it proceeded uneventfully. I was dead tired landing in Valencia,

Spain. The only thing I knew about Valencia was Valencia oranges, the best oranges in the world, thin-skinned and full of juice. At home I had been making the Brazilian drink known as "Sucre de L'Orange", a concoction made of orange juice, spun in a mixer with sugar and ice. I could kill for one right now.

I went through customs and rented a car. I made sure to purchase additional insurance and picked up a road map. It was confusing. I headed out of the airport and located a main artery which appeared to be headed in the right direction. My final destination was Requena, a town about 100 kilometers away. I was not used to Spanish road signs and, almost immediately I got lost. I found myself driving through narrow streets between ancient buildings. Old women dressed in black walked in the streets. I was to discover that if a woman in Spain were widowed, she would wear black the rest of her life. Incredible…They looked at me suspiciously and I backed off.

I retraced my steps and found the main road. My judgment was compromised by lack of sleep, but this time, I felt confident that I was headed in the right direction. I passed large orchards with orange trees. There they were…Huge piles of Valencia oranges…I couldn't wait to taste them…But that was not to be. These oranges were being exported to the U.K. for orange marmalade, of all things. No one in Spain drank orange juice for breakfast. In fact, no one in Spain even ate breakfast. I once asked for orange juice and got something like Tang, a powdered orange drink…What a waste of a national resource…

I continued on…The highway quickly degenerated into a three lane road, which was extremely common in Spain, with the center, "suicide lane" meant for passing. I would soon experience this at first hand. Today, I just wanted to get to Requena and get some sleep. My car was a Ciat, the Spanish version of the Italian Fiat, only worse. With its 0.9 liter engine it could barely pull the hills in high gear and I was now entering a very mountainous region. I had never heard of a car with an engine displacement that began with a "0", but now I was driving one.

It turned out that most cars and trucks in Spain used tiny engines in order to save fuel, which averaged about three to four times the cost in the U.S. The end result was that no one could go up the hills with any speed, which is why the passing lane was so popular…Maybe a little too popular….

I slowed for the tank truck ahead of me. It looked like a gasoline truck with dual trailers. As I got closer, I looked for some identification. On the back of one tank, in large letters, I could read the word "VINO". As I was to learn, "vino" was the national beverage in Spain, so much so that it was consumed almost as soon as it was produced, giving it a very raw taste. The aging process for wine was non-existent, as far as I could tell, and what little aging there was probably occurred in these tank trucks on the way to market. Usually, local wine was served with "Agua Con Gasa", or carbonated water. It was customary to dilute it 1:1 for consumption… Actually, the Rioja region in Northern Spain did produce better wines, but most people just drank the local version because it was cheaper and more readily available. Every town in Spain had its own winery, for better or for worse…

I was now approaching Requena. I located a downtown hotel and checked in. The buildings were ancient and had been repaired numerous times over the centuries. I was tired but, worse, I was hungry. I had eaten a small breakfast on the SAS flight coming in to Copenhagen, but that was hours ago. I walked around town…I found two restaurants, but both were closed. No one spoke English in this small town. In desperation I went to a local bar and ordered a beer, and then another. I looked at the appetizers on the bar, which were known as Tapas. I could not recognize anything…I picked at a few things that looked like cheese, but I left most of it untouched. I finally just went back to the hotel and went to bed.

The next morning I was contacted by the hotel manager. I had a call on the hallway phone…I picked it up and it was Becky, an engineer from General Electric who was assigned to the Cofrentes nuclear project. I asked her where I could get breakfast. I explained that I had not eaten in 24 hours. She laughed. "Stay where you are", she said, "I'll pick you up". She drove me to her house and prepared some French toast. I was greatly appreciative. Slowly, I was to learn about the rural Spanish lifestyle...

As it turned out, Francisco Franco had been the dictator in Spain from 1936 until his death in 1975, just seven years before. As Wikipedia explained: "After the end of World War II, Franco maintained his control in Spain through the implementation of austere measures: the systematic suppression of dissident views through censorship and coercion, the imprisonment of ideologically opposed enemies in concentration camps throughout the country, the implementation of forced labor in prisons, and the use of the death penalty and heavy prison sentences as deterrents for his ideological enemies".

Slowly, Spain was recovering in the Post-Franco era, but very little of it had touched Requena. Franco viewed himself a "the defender of Catholic Spain", so 98% of the citizens were Catholic. The customs in this village could only be described as "quaint". In retrospect, they had only been connected to electrical power for the last 15 years, so their situation was somewhat understandable. Looking out over the farmers' fields, I could see men behind horse-drawn plows; it could just as easily been 1882 or even 1782 instead of 1982. The only clue that it was not the 18th century was the presence of pneumatic tires on the horse-drawn carts...

But I needed to get to work. Becky was going in later, so she took me back to the hotel and gave me directions to get to the plant, built in a river valley some 30 kilometers distant. I thanked her for breakfast and departed. It was a beautiful drive through rolling hills, taking the better part of an hour. As I approached the valley, the road switched back and forth down a very steep grade until, several miles later, it ran alongside the river. The nuclear reactor at Cofrentes had been located in an uninhabited part of Spain, and probably for a good reason, I thought to myself. Suddenly, I came across an ancient bridge that was just wide enough for one car. No one was coming from the other direction, so I sped across. From the appearance of the stonework, it appeared to be a Roman bridge, constructed just wide enough for two chariots to cross. Unfortunately, no one drove a chariot anymore. I couldn't believe that, 2000 years later, it was still possible to drive over it. What an engineering feat! I always wondered how the Romans could possibly build these complex structures using something as clumsy as the Roman numeral system…

My thoughts were interrupted as I rounded a bend and caught a glimpse of the twin cooling tours of the nuclear power plant. I pulled into the parking lot, grabbed my toolbox, and headed into the security area. And then the difficulty began. In Catholic Spain, a "middle name" was assigned at confirmation, when a person officially joined the church, usually at age 12 or so. But that name was never used in official documents. The security guard was annoyed. I couldn't understand what he was saying as he examined my passport. Then he took a ball point pen and "crossed off" my middle name. He was defacing my passport…I objected but it was too late. I hoped that wouldn't nullify the whole document…

And then I waited…a half hour went by. Nothing. Finally, a General Electric engineer showed up. I got into his car. We proceeded to the business offices of GE on site and went through the "badging process", which took another twenty minutes or so. The plant was still in the construction phase so security with outside contractors had many layers to it. Later, I discovered a much more efficient way to enter the plant. I would drive into the plant at 7:00 a.m., before the GE people in the business office arrived and tell the security guard "El Jefe de Torno", which meant the "Chief of the Turns" or, in English, The Shift Supervisor. At the nuclear plant, after hours, El Jefe de Torno was God. He had total control over everything, so when the security guard called him, he would immediately authorize my entrance. That saved at least an hour a day…

But today was my first day. I proceeded to the offices of the Spanish company, Hidroelectrica Espanola, where the processor of the 4010 computer system had been set up in a room behind the main business area. This was going to be a challenge. The first task was going to be the expansion of memory, requiring a major wire-wrapping effort. I got to work. Memory was extremely sensitive to electrical "noise", so every memory signal had to be wrapped with 30 gauge "twisted pair". One wire was for the signal, while the other was a ground wire twisted around the first wire for noise rejection and connected to signal common. Basically, it was twice the work.

By noon, I was getting hungry but I had no way of asking anyone about lunch. I had noticed a sort of "sandwich bar" across the street, so I went over and got a coke and a sandwich, consisting of a few slices of meat on a hard roll. Not very satisfying…I went back to work…. Surprisingly, I found people sleeping at their desks. I had to pass through the office to get to the computer room, which irritated the snoozers to no end. They made their grievances known to me in no uncertain terms …In the future I tried to be as quiet as possible…

It took me a while to fully understand the nature of life in this region of Spain. Everything was based upon the temperature. Without electricity and air conditioning, everyday existence had turned into a "heat avoidance" mentality. Breakfast was never served anywhere…Workers would arrive early in the morning after having only a cup of coffee and then work until noon, at which time they would take a two to three hour "lunch break" mid-day. It was common to go to the local restaurant, outside the gates, at lunch time and have a few beers. A large lunch would be served, along with wine, followed by some "after dinner" drinks. Office workers would then go back to the plant and sleep at their desks in the mid-day heat until at 2:30 or 3:00 p.m. They would then work until about 7:00 p.m. and go home. But it was still too hot, even then, to eat. Finally, around 10:30 p.m. or so, restaurants would open and customers would arrive for a very light dinner, usually consisting of a "tortilla", which, to Spaniards, meant an omelet, served cold…

I lost ten pounds over the next two weeks until I figured out the schedule. Finally I decided to go out with the other contractors at noon, but I would not touch the alcohol. No one could understand why until one of them stopped by one day to pick me up for lunch. He walked into the computer room where I was busy wire wrapping tiny wires on the computer backpanel. He laughed out loud…"Oh", he exclaimed, waving his arms, "now I understand". We both laughed…

But getting back to the motel was sometimes a problem. If a left at the wrong time, I would find myself behind the "workers' bus" with its tiny diesel engine. The bus would slowly wind its way up the hill above the river in low gear. If I got behind it, I could add easily another half-hour to the trip home. This time I was going to beat the bus before it got to the grade, so I down-shifted my 0.9 liter Ciat into third gear, floored the accelerator, and pulled out to pass on the flat area along the river. Unfortunately, I had not yet learned the unwritten rules of driving in Spain.

In the first place, Spanish men were extremely concerned with their masculinity, and that applied to their driving as well. Their heroes were the bull fighters, the ultimate in machismo, who appeared in the rings built in every town: "Las Corridas de Toros". So, to pass a man on the road was to insult his manhood. And secondly, to pass a truck or bus was even a greater insult. As I was soon to learn, commercial vehicles always had the right of way, no matter what. I had heard the story of a GE engineer approaching a Roman bridge near the Cofrentes site. There was only room for one vehicle at a time to cross but the engineer thought he could make it across before a bus entered the bridge from the opposite direction. He was wrong. The bus sped up and the engineer had no choice but to drive his car off the road into the ditch. Luckily, he missed the bridge abutment, which would have killed him. The rental car was totaled.

And so I pressed on the gas pedal, slowly gaining on the workers' bus. As I pulled alongside on a two-lane road, the driver sped up, blowing his horn in an attempt to keep me from passing. We battled, side by side. I could see a car rapidly approaching in my lane, so it was now or never. I shifted into high gear and with inches to spare I managed to pass the bus and pull into the right hand lane …It was way too close for comfort. I had no idea the driver would actually try to prevent me from passing…I always had to learn these lessons the hard way…

I arrived back at the hotel. I hated to wait until ten o'clock for dinner but I had no choice. I had located a new restaurant on the outskirts of town, so I decided to give it a try. I arrived exactly at ten and found myself to be the first customer. I walked between two large dogs, sprawled on the cool tile floor in the entry way and took a seat. The menu was completely in Spanish, so I had to do a lot of guessing. The menus were totally unlike the menus to which I was accustomed in Mexican restaurants; there were no enchiladas or burritos…I did recognize the word Camarones, and I knew it meant shellfish. I also knew that Gambas was the word for "shrimp". Cerveza was a no-brainer, so I ordered "Cerveza y Gambas". The waiter looked puzzled…"Gambas?" he said…I was beginning to have some doubts…"Si", I said in my best ninth-grade Spanish. He shrugged his shoulders and left.

The beer came first, and as usual, it was delicious, especially after spending all day in the heat of the power plant. And then came the Gambas, a huge platter of shrimp with heads and tails on…That was it…By this time I didn't care…I think I ate the tails, shell and all…

Finally, the weekend was upon me. And unlike weekends to come, when I would work 12 hours a day, this time I decided to take time off. It was Saturday…I put on my running clothes and went out for a jog in the late afternoon. The road wound through farmers' fields and into the countryside. Finally, I reached a turning-around point and headed home. As I neared the hotel, I noticed that the town was filled with people, out in the cool of the evening in their finest clothes, walking around the town square. It was "El Paseo", a tradition passed down for hundreds of years. For the youth, it was the basis of courtship. Young girls, dressed to the nines, giggled at me in my running clothes as they promenaded past the hotel, on their way to the "Helado", or ice cream stand. I stood out like a sore thumb…

Now it was Sunday. I was starving…I walked out of the hotel and stood on the steps. Suddenly, I was startled by loud explosions. I looked to my left…People were marching out of the Catholic Church with loaves of bread on their head, throwing firecrackers. I had absolutely no idea what kind of religious celebration this represented. Later, I called it "The Festival of Bread on Head with Fireworks" as I tried to explain it to my family.

Hunger was gnawing at me. Absolutely no restaurants were open. I walked around town. Churchgoers were lining up in front of an open-air stand to buy some kind of food. I had no idea what it was, but I immediately got in line. As I got closer, I could see that the proprietors were squeezing what looked like bread dough into a number ten can of boiling oil, heated by a charcoal fire. I finally got to the head of the line…They were making churros…There was a pause in production…Apparently the fire had gone out so it was necessary to re-light it. Production resumed and the churro was removed from the hot oil and covered with sugar. I put down a few Pesetas and took ownership. It was delicious, although slightly oily….

As I entered the hotel I began to feel ill. I immediately knew the problem…the oil had been too cold and it had penetrated the churro. Normally, when food is cooked in hot oil, the oil sears and cooks the outside. If the oil is too cold, it penetrates the food and the food becomes unpalatable. In my efforts to avoid starvation, I had poisoned myself…I felt miserable the rest of the day…

Finally, it was Monday of the second week and I was headed back to the site in the early morning hours. After being off work for two days, I had forgotten a necessary turn, so I branched off on a side road. As I proceeded, I began to notice that things seemed unfamiliar. Suddenly I cleared a ridge and there before me was a medieval city, totally abandoned. I stopped the car and got out. The rising sun shone through the broken window casements and illuminated the towers and collapsed masonry, casting long shadows… It was absolutely still… There was no other human being in sight…I cannot describe the eeriness of that moment… I felt as if I had been transported to another age.

But I was going to be late…My mind slipped back to more mundane thoughts as I turned my car around and headed back towards the intersection. I picked up the main road and continued to the plant, where I checked in with security. My job was going well and I proceeded to the computer room, anxious to finish the first phase of my project. Several hours passed. Now the office people were at work and I was being summoned. As a foreigner, the Spanish company insisted that I be examined by a medical doctor for communicable diseases. I was somewhat offended by the insinuation that I might have a communicable disease, but I swallowed my feelings and went ahead to the onsite medical establishment where I was poked and prodded and a medical history taken. I was diagnosed with mild hypertension and given some hydrochlorothiazide to take. Other than that, I was good to go…

I received my official stamp of good health and returned to my job. It would do no good to question authority, I discovered. I was starting to learn the basics of life in Spain. Franco had ruled the country for almost 40 years with an iron fist, dealing severely with dissidents. Even now, people were not used to questioning authority; they appeared to be quite comfortable with, and to even expect, a life of top-down decision making… I had been advised by my GE sponsors that life in Spain, and particularly life in a nuclear plant, requires abiding by the rules at all times.

And then they told me the story…One of the GE engineers had reported to a power plant site in Spain and discovered two large turbines sitting on blocks out in the yard. Apparently the bearings were bad, and they had destroyed the turbines, but he couldn't get the whole story. Finally it came out. The plant had gone into a shutdown and the engineers had examined the bearings on the turbines and found them to be in need of replacement. Management had disagreed and ordered the plant started up. Shortly afterwards the bearings failed, wiping out the turbines. When the engineer asked why he had spun up the turbines under those conditions, the worker replied, "When the Chief of the Plant asks you to do something, to die would not be enough".

I couldn't believe it…That kind of thinking violated every fiber of my being…But I put the thought aside and continued with my work. I was now reaching a "stopping point". I had upgraded the eight-year-old 4010 processor to modern standards. The next step would be to move it to the computer room in the reactor building, where it would eventually be mated with analog and digital input and output cabinets, data links, and a video system. There was nothing more I could do at the moment. Rather than have me wait around at Honeywell's high labor rates, GE management decided that it was less expensive to send me home until they were prepared for the next phase of the project. I did not know it at the time, but this project would require seven more trips…

I was glad to go home. I had managed to re-schedule my itinerary so that I could take an Iberia flight from Valencia to Madrid, a TWA 747 flight from Madrid to New York, and a TWA 747 flight from New York to Seattle. I was a happy camper, except, of course, for the Iberia flight which was "space available".

The next morning I headed out to the Valencia airport. I was running late and the traffic was miserable. There was a considerable amount of mountain road between Requena and the Mediterranean Coast and the trucks were creeping in low gear up the inclines, slowing everyone down. But there was the wide open middle lane. I could tell that it was illegal to pass but creeping along behind these trucks was killing my time…So, I down shifted into third gear and went for it. I was doing well…I had managed to pass all the trucks on the hill…And then I saw the Policia on motorcycles…

They pulled me over and with great bureaucratic efficiency, proceeded to write me a ticket. As I was to discover, crafting official government documents was an art form, passed down from generation to generation in European countries, and this was no exception. Carefully, on the seat of his motorcycle, the police officer composed the document. Minutes went by…my blood pressure was through the roof. Finally, he handed me the ticket…It was a masterpiece…The script was perfect. Would I go to jail or have to appear before a judge? I could not tell… Finally he pointed to a number on the document. "Pesetas", he said. It was a modest amount and I offered to pay it on the spot. I was hoping they did not think I was bribing them…No…They accepted the amount and then insisted on carefully writing me a receipt…I could have screamed..

I thanked them and got back into my car. It was really getting late and I pushed as fast as I could legally go, and a little bit more. I was now on the coastal plain approaching the Valencia airport. I turned in my car and got in line. Finally, I was at the counter. The Iberia Airlines agent took one look at my ticket and told me that the TWA flight from Madrid to New York had been canceled. This had to be a huge lie…I had just checked with TWA in Madrid and everything was on schedule. But the agent was very friendly. "Don't worry", he said, I can get you on an Iberia flight from Madrid to New York". The old hustle…I couldn't believe it. I insisted on retaining my TWA reservation. "But the flight is canceled", he repeated, sounding very peeved. "I know", I said, "I'll just make arrangements when I get there". He had lost that particular fight, but he still had one more trick up his sleeve. "OK", he said, but the Iberia flight to Madrid is full". "You will have to fly first class". At this point, I could have cared less. As we climbed out over the Mediterranean I sat back in my first class seat enjoying an early morning cocktail. My cares were over… In Madrid I would be connecting with TWA Boeing 747's all the way back to Seattle…

Or so I thought…I arrived in Madrid and waited for my 12:30 flight, which, I was assured, was on schedule. We were still sitting in the boarding area when it became time to board the aircraft…Still there was no announcement. I could see the aircraft at the end of the jetway, so what was the problem? I went up to the desk…Apparently there was mechanical problem…I waited…An hour went by…Passengers were grumbling…The man behind me was becoming irritated and I could overhear his conversation. He had been through this before…And he was getting mad…

TWA, he claimed, was stalling…In those days airlines overbooked their flights, anticipating that cancellations would take care of the extra passengers. Sometimes the cancellations would not materialize, which left the airline facing a thousand dollar per passenger penalty for those who were denied a seat on international flights. There were strict regulations about this in the U.S., but in foreign countries, he claimed, airlines played fast and loose with the rules. The strategy, according to him, was for the airline to claim a "malfunction" and stall. Eventually, passengers would get fed up with waiting and change their reservations to other airlines; in this case the other airline was Iberia…

When enough passengers had defected, he stated, the "malfunction" would suddenly be repaired and those remaining passengers would be seated, thus saving the airline the cost of the penalty. I had never heard this story before, but I had also never heard of a 747 at the gate with a mechanical problem. Finally, several hours later, we departed for New York. By the time we arrived, we had all missed our domestic flight connections, so we were given coupons for a local motel and meals. The idea of staying in an airport motel did not appeal to me, so I called my father in Westfield, New Jersey to come and pick me up. I stayed at home in my old bedroom and had a chance to spend some time with my parents. The next day my father drove me back to JFK and I took a flight back to Seattle.

Weeks went by…I lapsed back into a normal routine…Until I got my next call. But this time, I was going to make my own reservations, and I was not going to stay in that crummy hotel in downtown Requena.

Furthermore, I was going to fly business class, which was authorized by GE for its own employees on foreign assignments. Bill, my boss from the old instrumentation group, hit the roof. Bill and I were still having our culture wars, so he insisted upon calling General Electric Nuclear Energy Division (GENED) in San Jose, California and asking to speak to the project manager for Cofrentes. After exchanging a few pleasantries, he got down to business. "Did you know", he said, "that Steve Buck is flying to Spain business class?" The project manager acknowledged that he did. Bill was flummoxed. He paused, trying to think of a comeback. He had it; "Did you realize that business class is costing one thousand dollars more than economy?" he said. "Yes", the project manager replied, "we think he's worth it". My boss was beside himself…The best he could come up with was a very weak, "Well, it's not Honeywell policy!" He was really mad…. In reality it made no difference at all. I would just invoice GE and GE would pass the costs on to the Spanish utility as part of the project billing. Eventually, Bill gave up and let me take care of business my own way. He only had one requirement; in his eyes, he was doing me a huge favor by letting me go overseas and he demanded something in return. He told me it was customary for employees on long trips to bring some sort of "tribute" to their bosses. I couldn't believe it…I was putting up with the most difficult challenges of my life on these trips, working extremely long hours, risking my life and invoicing the customer $30,000 or $40,000 a visit, which would go against Bill's bottom line, making the Seattle office the number one branch in earnings in the Western Region. So I owed him? But I still liked Bill; he always gave me good raises and supported me against attacks from upper management. What else could you ask for in a manager? Bill's only problem was that he was just suffering from a pre-computer age mindset. So, thereafter, I always brought him a box of Spanish cigars or Spanish sherry every time I returned from Cofrentes. We declared a truce…When he retired, several years later, I would begin to experience major problems with management…Somehow I always ended up being the nail that stuck up and got hammered…

Luckily, Bill did not really know the details of my flights to Spain in those days or he would have had a screaming fit. What I had done was to sign up for TWA's brand new frequent flyer program. In the early days of TWA frequent flyer programs you could get away with the most unbelievable things. I would buy a ticket to Spain on business class and then show them my frequent flyer card, which would get me any instant upgrade to first class for no points. And if I was flying internationally first class, I would be automatically upgraded to first class on the domestic leg. I was flying in the lap of luxury. But it got even better. When I upgraded to first class, it doubled the amount of points that I received per flight mile. Years later I was able to use those points to take my wife to Australia, Portugal, Spain, Greece, and England. And if I flew overseas with TWA in the first three months of the year, when air travel was down, I would be given a free domestic roundtrip ticket for any destination. As busy as I was, I had no opportunity to use the free ticket, which expired at the end of May. There was no way I was going to let the opportunity go to waste, so I decided, on Sunday of the Memorial Day weekend, to fly, roundtrip, from Seattle to JFK. Using my frequent flyer card I was able to upgrade the free ticket to first class for no points, which doubled my miles. I enjoyed the champagne breakfast and landed in New York at about 3:00 p.m. I then turned around and took the next TWA first class flight back to Seattle for a steak and wine dinner. The whole free trip gave me about 10,000 miles on my frequent flyer account, and I got to see two movies....What a way to run an airline... or maybe I should say, in 2012, an ex-airline...

Days went by...GE called, and I was back on the road again. The only bad part of my trip was landing in Madrid at 7:30 a.m. local time and having to wait until 3:30 for my Iberia flight to Valencia. I would be dead tired, not having gotten any sleep on the plane, so I would doze off in my chair at the airport until my flight was called. But it was difficult to hear the flight announcement and interpret the gate number...When I really got hungry I would visit the airport restaurant.

Unfortunately, the only thing the restaurant offered was the cold, plain "tortilla" so I would have that and a Coke. Yuk…

I returned to the plant. Now things were getting more difficult and I was running out of spare parts. Unfortunately, if I let GE order the parts, they would take days if not weeks to show up and would often get "hung up" in customs, requiring manual intervention to release them. I could not afford to pause the installation process for this to happen…It was taking long enough as it was… so I devised a plan.

Before I left for Spain, I would order the parts I needed next-day-air from the Honeywell Depot in Chicago to my home in Washington State. I would put them in a large carry-on bag which I purchased for that very purpose. I called it my "smuggler's bag". The strategy was very simple. Baggage was always routed to the final destination, which was Valencia, where it would go through a customs inspection. I would carry my smugglers bag off the plane in Madrid with the circuit boards I needed and walk right by security personnel to the domestic wing, where I would wait for my Iberia flight to Valencia. I would always manage to be the first off the plane in Valencia, where I would grab my bag and run to the car rental agency. I would rent a car, run out to the parking lot and dump my bag into the trunk and then return to the baggage claim area where my luggage and toolbox were being searched by customs officials. Sometimes customs would hold my Tektronix scope and not let it enter the country; other times they would try to confiscate my cassette tapes and player. Often, I would have to get GE engineers to go down to Valencia and get items released; a chore they did not enjoy. On one occasion, customs refused to release my toolbox and I had to use the customer's until I recovered my own as I left the country…The custom agents' actions had become extremely unpredictable. But no matter what, I always managed to get the circuit boards in my smuggler's bag into the country…

I was starting to learn some of the survival techniques in Spain. I had now located a motel just outside Requena that actually had a restaurant.

I could get a cup of coffee in the morning and a minimalistic sort of pastry in a bag. But the best thing was; I could work late at the plant as long as I arrived back at the restaurant by 10:30 p.m. or so for dinner. I had fallen in love with Emperador or swordfish, which was cheap and plentiful in Spain. The motel had a special dish of swordfish pieces cooked up in a tomato sauce that was absolutely wonderful, so I had it almost every night, along with a few beers, which I consumed in a very short period of time. Sometimes the waiter would wait several feet away from me with a beer bottle behind his back so he didn't have to run back to the bar for a second one...

But the motel, as I was to learn, had two seasons: Hot and Cold. In the summer, the tile floors were cool and comfortable. There was no air conditioning, but the combination of the tile floors and the breeze blowing through the open windows made the rooms very pleasant. In winter, the opposite was true. The tile floors were like ice. Electricity was a relatively new phenomenon in this part of Spain so it was heavily rationed. If I left the room at 5:30 a.m. with even one of the 25 watt light bulbs on, the manager would yell at me. And he would never turn on the electric heat until someone rented a room. This meant that, in winter the rooms were icy cold. Slowly the room would warm...The heat would eventually rise so that it felt fairly normal when you walked in. But when you crawled into bed you entered the sub arctic zone... It took a week in winter for the room to become warm all the way down to the tile floor...And the restaurant was equally cold...At five a.m. in the morning the motel manager would ride his bicycle to the restaurant and build a wood fire in a stove in the middle of the room. We would huddle around the stove and wait for an espresso to warm us up...

As the days passed I became friendly with some of the other contractors, who were also staying in Requena. One day, I volunteered to drive them to a new restaurant we discovered just on the outskirts of town. Passing through Requena was difficult at best. Ancient cobblestone streets intersected with concrete roadways with serious potholes. I was slowly following a local person in a small car who, as best as I could tell, was creeping along at about ten miles an hour looking for a parking spot. I shifted down and passed him, thinking nothing of it. Then I remembered…that machismo thing…I looked back in the rearview mirror and I could see him accelerating towards me. He rocketed past the car and then came to a halt at an intersection. He jumped out of his car and began waving his arms and screaming at me. "What is he saying?', I asked the others. "You don't want to know", they replied. "They think you are a German". I laughed. "He is mad because you passed him". Finally he got back in his car and left. We turned into the highway and headed to the restaurant. We went into the bar and, suddenly, there he was, the explosive person, having a drink and chatting with a woman next to him. "Uh-oh" I thought to myself. But he totally ignored me…Spanish men and women, I was to discover, could suddenly explode in anger and, just as suddenly, calm down….

One day followed another. At the reactor site, the project was entering a new phase. The computer had been installed in the reactor building and the half dozen input/output cabinets had been hauled up from the warehouse to be connected to the system. Rats had gnawed some of the wiring on the video system and the CRT's on the videos had not been energized since 1975. In fact, none of the equipment stored in the warehouse had been powered up since it left Phoenix some eight years prior. I had my work cut out for me…Parts were in short supply… I could not always anticipate what I needed in advance, so when I had an urgent need, I would have parts shipped, on an emergency basis, directly from Chicago to the airport in Valencia, where I would drive down and pick them up.

It was on such a winter night that I left the site after work and headed towards Valencia. I had never driven the road at night, and it was terrifying. It was absolutely pitch dark with no street lighting and the traffic was moving very rapidly over the narrow mountain roads. Curves would suddenly appear without warning. I had to pay absolute attention to my driving. I rounded a corner at 60 miles an hour and there it was…two cars had collided head-on in the center "suicide lane". The driver of the nearest car was in a state of shock. He stumbled out of his crushed vehicle right in front of me. In the corner of my eye I caught the movement and, instantaneously, I swerved my car off the road to the right, barely missing him. When I pulled the car back on the pavement I tried to look back but, in the darkness, I could not tell what was happening. If I had hit him, I would have been immediately arrested. No one could have intervened in my behalf; I would have been left to rot in a Spanish prison...

My heart was racing...What should I do? I didn't dare stop in this traffic...My mind flashed back to a story I had heard in Poland about a European contractor who had rented a car. In those days in Poland, the roadway was shared by pedestrians, bicycles and horse-drawn carts. He had inadvertently killed a pedestrian. His passport was taken and he was still in prison. In a foreign country, civil rights can be non-existent, as I was shortly to learn. I continued to Valencia and picked up my parts...And then I remembered the story of a Honeywell specialist in Saudi Arabia...The first advice he had been given was this: If you get in a car accident, abandon the car and run away as fast as possible...I was beginning to understand that reasoning...

I picked up my parts in Valencia and returned to Requena. Slowly the computer system was coming together...I was now taking a little time off to explore the area. When my wife found out that the Lladro pottery factory was in Valencia, my fate was sealed, and every trip required that I bring home some figurines. Driving to the Valencia airport was bad enough, but finding the pottery factory in the middle of town was impossible. I did succeed once, with much difficulty, but this time I was going to just drive to the airport and take a cab.

That plan worked out reasonably well. I could tell the driver "Lladro" on the way in, and "Aeropuerto" on the way out and let him negotiate the crowded streets. He got me to the factory and I browsed through the shop...Even in Spain, the first quality figurines were expensive, but in the "seconds" part of the retail store, I could purchase items with small defects for a very reasonable price. I made my selection, had them packed in straw for transport and returned to the cab, waiting outside. "Aeropuerto", I pronounced in my best Spanish. The driver corrected me:…"AeroPUERto, no AeroPORTo". I stood corrected…I was glad I was being tutored…Some day I might have to know Spanish just to live in the U.S.A., I thought to myself…I just wish my father had not forced me to take two years of French in high school instead of Spanish…He told me that it was "the language of diplomacy". Unfortunately I never got to be a diplomat or go to France, at least not on business…

I headed back towards my motel. I had almost given up finding a decent restaurant in Requena and was resigning myself to my usual fate when I suddenly remembered a conversation with some of the GE engineers who had discovered a medieval restaurant half way between Valencia and Requena. I decided to find it and stop for dinner. "How could this possibly be a medieval restaurant?" I thought to myself. But they were right…When I walked in I could see that the entire round dining area was a giant chimney, slowly tapering to a stack at the top. In the center of the floor a fire burned without benefit of surrounding fireplace. Tables were arranged around the fire, which was the only source of warmth… and smoke…Actually, the smoke was not too bad and I ordered steak with Bechamel sauce…It was delicious.

I was feeling much better about my travels in Spain, despite the near-misses. The system was slowly coming to life and at least I was getting enough nutrition to keep from feeling starved all the time. I was preparing to leave for Thanksgiving when I got the news from the GE onsite manager. "The Consejo is coming", he said. The Consejo was the Consejo de Seguridad Nuclear, the Spanish version of our Nuclear Regulatory Commission, or NRC. They were inspecting the site in preparation for loading nuclear fuel. This was really a big deal… GE could not let me go home lest there be some problem with the computer which would cause them to fail the inspection. "But it's Thanksgiving", I complained. I had previously smuggled in two bags of cranberries for the manager's wife who was desperate to have a real Thanksgiving dinner. The Spanish lead engineer heard my complaints. "Hey", he said, "we have turkeys in Spain!" Thanks a lot, I thought to myself... The GE site manager took me into his private office and closed the door. "You have to stay", he said, "I will give you anything you want"...

I was stunned...What did I want? No one had ever asked me that question before. I stared at him trying to figure out an answer. Finally, I had it...If they wanted me that badly, I would just stay and work. I told him that Thursday and Friday would be invoiced to him at holiday rates...He just shrugged his shoulders. "OK" he said, and we shook hands.

So that is how I came to work over Thanksgiving. I called my wife and she was very upset. We were planning to join her parents for a holiday at Cannon Beach, Oregon, a yearly tradition. I reassured her that I would have some presents for her from Valencia, and she guessed immediately that they would be Lladro figurines. She was right...

So the Consejo came and inspected the site and found everything to be satisfactory for loading nuclear fuel. I spent the better part of the holiday performing alignment and convergence procedures on the ancient video tubes that we had pulled out of the warehouse, at least on the ones that actually "fired up" and worked. There was just one problem: even after my best efforts, the Spanish customer rejected the video displays as inferior, insisting on the newer, High Resolution tubes that Honeywell was using on the latest computer systems. Honeywell would purchase the tubes from the original manufacturer, mark them up and sell them to General Electric, who would mark them up even further and sell them to the Spanish utility. When the Spanish technician I was working with found about the new order for tubes, he was appalled.. "I can't believe it", he would complain, "One channel and no sound for $6,000". All I could do was laugh...

Finally the visit from the Consejo was over and I was allowed to leave. I packed my bags and headed for Valencia to go home. I was flying this time to Madrid on an Iberia Boeing 727 with rear airstair, which we used in the absence of jetways. My arms were bulging with Lladros in bags stuffed with straw packing. I was really worried that they would not let me take them on board so I made a plan to be at the head of the line, run up the rear airstairs and stuff the Lladros into the small closet space available at the rear of the aircraft. The flight was announced for boarding, and as per plan I raced up the stairs and shoved all the bags into the tiny closets.

"No, No, No", the flight attendant admonished me. My heart sunk. "But I thought these closets were for passenger stowage?" I asked her. "Yes", she answered, "But first it is necessary to ask!" I was embarrassed. Once again I had violated protocol but I didn't care. At least the Lladros were safe. I had learned well the old Honeywell adage, "It is better to beg forgiveness than to ask permission". I knew that once I got to Madrid, the bins on the 747's were large enough to accommodate the Lladros safely…Quickly, I took my seat…I had picked up a Valencia newspaper with an article about the Cofrentes Nuclear Power Plant. With my limited Spanish, I could tell that the article was informing the public that the plant was well ahead of schedule and was in "low power testing". I couldn't believe it…we hadn't even loaded nuclear fuel yet! I shook my head in dismay…Propaganda was obviously a world-wide art form…

Finally, I arrived back in Seattle. Everyone at home was very pleased with the Lladros…I could relax for a while…And then GE was on the phone…I had only been home for several weeks, and it was nearing Christmas, but duty called…I would be working with the GE engineer from San Jose who planned to load, install and test new software. The project still had a ways to go but there was light at the end of tunnel. When I reported to the site I recognized Jim, an engineer from Phoenix with whom I had worked in the past. I was surprised to see him…and then the plot began to unfold.

Jim had been hired away from Honeywell by GETSCO, the General Electric Technical Services Company. He had relocated overseas and was now taking on computer contracts in Europe. The pressure had been intense from GE to get Honeywell out of the Cofrentes site and hire GETSCO field engineers, so, although he did not admit it, he was here to take my job. However, the GE manager on site had resisted, and it looked like I was going to be able to complete the installation. Although Jim would not say so, I guessed that his purpose today was to evaluate the site and to take it under maintenance contract once I finished the installation. I was OK with that. His wife had accompanied him on the trip, and she was now staying at my motel, so I agreed to drive Jim to and from work so that his wife could use the car.

I walked over and met the software engineer from GENED in San Jose. And then I discovered that the software installation was not quite going as planned. The new operating system had been punched onto several decks of IBM cards.. The only problem was, they would not load into the computer. The procedure was to load the Minimum Loader with the card reader. The Minimum Loader would then load the System Loader, which would load the operating system software. The problem was, the Minimum Loader would not load the System Loader. The GE software engineer was "dead in the water". I tried every trick in the book…No luck…Sometimes card punches could be "out of registration" in that the holes punched in the data cards were slightly out of position. That did not appear to be the case. Finally, in desperation, after hours of failures, I made the decision to alter the standard Honeywell software by replacing a "jump not ready" instruction in the Mini Loader with a "no-op" or no operation. The card reader took off and began to read cards…We were home free…almost…

Unfortunately, the hardware problems continued. The upgraded computer system required more power than the site had originally planned, so we began to "push the limit" on the motor-generator set that powered the system. This was an early mechanical version of the UPS or Uninterruptible Power Supply, in which an AC generator, an AC motor and a DC motor were all connected on the same shaft. Incoming plant power would run the AC motor which would run the AC generator which would supply power to the system and charge, through rectifiers, a row of batteries. If incoming power failed, the DC motor would pick up and run the AC generator from batteries, powering the computer system. Unfortunately, the UPS had been sized for the original installation in 1975 and not the upgraded installation in 1983. I took the site engineers down to the basement and showed them the motor generator and the specifications. I told them that they were at the 150 ampere limit of the system. I got absolutely nowhere. Engineers from the utility would stare at the drawings and point out that Honeywell had specified a 150 ampere MG set. To them, if it was written in a drawing, it was "set in stone". No one would acknowledge that the UPS was being overloaded. How could it be? It was exactly the one that Honeywell had supplied…This was going nowhere…I had to find a way to reduce power consumption to prevent the system from tripping out…This was just like Apollo 13, except I didn't have any duct tape…I was frustrated out of my mind…Eventually I found a way to keep power consumption just barely within limits…

Every problem presented huge obstacles. All of the electrical hardware on the computer was U.S. standard while all of the electrical fittings on site were European. I ended up bringing a supply of U.S. fittings with me which embarrassed my hosts…Sometimes the problems were so difficult that I had to move away from the computer to think about them. Usually, I would end up locking myself in the bathroom just to get away and think in peace. Often that worked…until the air conditioning broke down. Immediately the chief engineer appeared in the computer room. He knew how sensitive the computer was to heat and his plan was to shut it down, which would have completely stopped my work. I couldn't let that happen, so I objected. He looked at me. "How much heat can the computer tolerate?" he asked. I looked at the huge Fahrenheit dial thermometer on the wall. I had to come up with a number. I really had no idea…"Ninety three degrees", I said, picking a number that I thought might be high enough to keep the system running but low enough, I hoped, to prevent any real damage to the computer..."OK", he said. I continued my work...The thermometer slowly began to climb...89, 90, 91...It paused...I was going to be OK....92..."Uh Oh", I thought to myself....And then it stopped rising...It hung at 92 degrees all afternoon until the air conditioning was restored that evening...Whew!

And so it continued. Even the upgraded memory in the 4010 processor was not sufficient to contain the entire operating system which, by now, had grown considerable larger than in 1975. To solve the problem, extra space on a Moving Head Disk Drive had to be utilized as virtual memory. And then there was the 090/190 data link problem. GE had developed its own small data acquisition system which communicated with our computer through an 090/190 parallel data link. But the communication on the GE end was based upon the original design of our data link boards circa 1975. By 1983, our data link boards had been upgraded and no longer communicated with GE's data system. The only solution was to downgrade the data link boards to an earlier hardware version...

Eventually, I reached a stopping point. The system was performing fairly well, despite numerous setbacks and I was preparing to go home for Christmas. I worked late that night to finish up. Finally, I was done...I picked up Jim and the two of us headed back towards Requena. It was pitch dark, but there was no traffic so the drive proceeded smoothly. Rounding a bend, I could see the motel lights ahead of us. I was dead tired. Jim was in the passenger seat and he and I were having a discussion about the site when I heard a "beep" behind me...It really did not register in my consciousness. I slowed and started a left turn into my hotel when WHAM! ...I felt a huge impact as the driver's side door caved in against my left arm...The car was thrown sideways...A bus, traveling at about 100 kilometers an hour had raked the side of my car with its protruding steel step. If I had been one-quarter of a second further into the turn, I would have been dead...The "beep" that I heard was from the bus telling me that he was "coming through" despite the fact that I had slowed down on the roadway ahead of him and was turning into the motel...

The bus pulled off the road and stopped. Both of the drivers' side doors were smashed in on my car so I had to crawl over and exit on the passenger side. The crash had apparently been witnessed by La Guardia Civil, which I did not realize until I stepped out of the car. La Guardia Civil or the Civil Guard was a remnant of Franco Spain. Their officers now patrolled highway areas in their funny gray hats and not-so-funny machine guns. In rural Spain, they were rumored to be "judge, jury, and executioner", so it was with some trepidation that I approached them. On the other hand, they were also thought to be the "people's police" interceding on the behalf of citizens against bureaucratic big government authority…I wasn't sure which way this was going to go… I could not understand the conversation as I approached the small group gathering at the roadside, but I recognized the motel owner and the bus driver. They were conversing with the Guardia Civil Officers.

Shortly we were all motioned inside the motel. We were going to have a trial, on the spot, conducted by La Guardia Civil. We stood motionless as the trial proceeded. The motel owner, to his credit, appeared to be acting as my defense attorney. The bus driver made his statement. The Guardia Civil officers then made their judgment, which, to the best of my understanding was either "no fault" or "fault on both sides" or something like that. The officers made a "wave off" motion with their hands and then a motion of tearing up a non-existent ticket. I thought I was off the hook…I proposed that we go to the bar for a drink…

Before I could leave, the motel owner grabbed my shoulder and proceeded to lecture me. He was extremely agitated and the dressing-down continued for several minutes. I looked at Jim, who had a serious expression on his face. The motel owner paused. "What he is telling you", said Jim "is that there are three classes of drivers in Spain. Truck drivers and bus drivers are the first class. When they are involved in an accident on the highway, they have no problems. Spanish citizens are the second class. When they are involved in an accident, they have some problems. Foreigners are the third class of drivers. When they are involved in an accident, they have MUCHAS PROBLEMAS". So that was it…I was lucky that the Guardia Civil had adjudicated the case. They had determined that there was fault on both sides, so there was no point in pursuing it further. They were the law and that was their decision….I was much relieved.

I was going home for Christmas… I was sick and tired of dealing with the Iberia Airline agents in Valencia, so I got up at 5:00 a.m. the next morning, determined to drive myself all the way to Madrid to catch my TWA flight. I crawled into the car from the passenger side and started it up…Everything worked…I put it in gear and headed towards Madrid. When I arrived, some three and a half hours later, I turned in the car and filled out an accident report. I had purchased insurance, so no one seemed concerned. Nevertheless, I exited the rental booth as rapidly as possible and headed into the terminal before anyone had a chance to inspect the damage…

I thoroughly enjoyed Christmas, but the threat of returning to Spain hung over my head. Sure enough, GE called again. I stalled as long as I could and then flew back to Spain. I checked in at the hotel. The owner was pleased to see me. I was his best customer. Then he proceeded to tell me the rest of the story, which I pieced together with my limited Spanish. As the motel owner related, a few hours after I departed for Madrid on the day after my crash, the Policia showed up. The Policia was the official bureaucratic law enforcement agency and apparently their jurisdiction overlapped with La Guardia. They intended to take my passport and jail me until such time as an official trial could be arranged. When they Policia asked about my whereabouts, the motel manager told them that I was no longer in the country. He explained it to me by making the same motion that I made every time I departed…The motion of a jet plane taking off from a runway…They were very annoyed…

I had no doubt as to what the outcome of that trial would have been… I was extremely lucky that this was my last trip…I just hoped that no one ratted me out to the Policia before I had a chance to make my Great Escape…

Volta Redonda

It was hot…and sticky: Miami Heat. It was 1982: It had taken me all day to travel from Seattle to Miami and was impossible to get a cab from the airport to my hotel. None of the cab drivers spoke English. Finally, I understood. I had to talk to the man standing on the sidewalk and tell him my destination. If he failed to communicate the information exactly to the driver, I would have no way of correcting him. I had no choice…

Unfortunately, in those days, I was unable to travel, in one day, from Seattle to Rio de Janeiro. Later, I was to tell one of my co-workers; "I couldn't believe it. I was flying to South America, and when I got off the plane, no one spoke one word of English". My friend looked at me and asked, "So where were you?" "Miami," I answered…Later, as I was to find out, the Spanish speakers referred to the city as "Mee-Om-Mee".

So much for bilingualism, I thought. Finally, I arrived at the hotel, where I was to meet Russ, my Honeywell traveling companion whom I was to educate in computer upgrade and troubleshooting operations and who planned to remain in Brazil for several months, as per the Honeywell agreement with CEMIG (Companhia Energetica de Minas Gerais), one of the largest hydroelectric energy suppliers in Brazil. It was now late evening. I checked into the hotel, but Russ was nowhere in sight.

I slept in the next morning. I went for breakfast, but still no Russ. "Well", I thought to myself, "I guess I'm just going to have to do this by myself". I was scheduled to be in Brazil for about a month, with two weeks spent at Brazilian National Steel (CSN or Companhia Siderurgica Nationale) in Volta Redonda and two weeks at the CEMIG San Simeon hydroelectric dam site. I had an evening departure, so, with nothing better to do, I went for a run…The hotel was near the airport; the air was pungent with the smell of jet fuel. Afterwards, I took a quick shower and packed my bags, heading for the airport and the departure of the VARIG, Brazilian Airlines flight at 8:30 p.m.

I arrived at the airport, walked through the entrance and headed towards my gate. There, standing in the foyer was a tall, youngish man wearing a cowboy hat…I knew instinctively that it must be Russ. I was right…I knew nothing about Russ, except that he was from Denver; but I was about to find out a whole lot more…

When I asked Russ about where he had been, I got some sort of evasive answer about "problems with my business visa", so I let it go at that. As I was to find out, after several Brazilian Antarctica beers, there was a whole lot more to the story than he had first admitted.

Russ was a lover-boy, as it turned out, looking for every out-of-town assignment as a way to find new, romantic adventure. The fact that he had a wife back in Denver seemed not to matter much in his scheme of things. As it turned out, Russ had just completed ten weeks of computer training at Honeywell in Phoenix and had used his time after hours to "hook up" with an airline stewardess who lived in Chicago and who frequented Phoenix on her flights.

What Russ had done, then, was to re-direct himself from Denver to Chicago, instead of Miami, for a night with his paramour. He had then flown down to Miami from Chicago that same day to meet me in the airport. I was later to be questioned intensively from the accounting department in Phoenix about why Russ claimed a Miami hotel cost on his expense report without submitting a receipt. When they asked me if I Russ had stayed in the hotel the previous night, I told them that the first time I had seen Russ was in the airport.

Russ really was a "loose cannon", I determined, but he was friendly enough and we enjoyed trading Honeywell stories on our departure from Miami. Unfortunately, the VARIG flight was one of the worst "milk runs" ever conceived in the annals of flight. Our first stop was in Caracas, Venezuela. The pilot of Airbus A-320 kept the air conditioning running while on the ground, so the stop was uneventful and comfortable. We departed Caracas after a short stay and headed south, into the wilds of South America.

Time passed slowly; looking out, I could see no lights in the darkness below. Finally, at 3:00 a.m. the cabin lights turned on and we prepared for a landing in what I thought was going to be Rio de Janeiro. The plane landed on the runway and moved to a taxi-way, where it stopped. The engines were shut down, as was the air-conditioning, and all doors were opened wide. I stared out the window…the jungle heat and humidity began to slowly displace the cool, dry air-conditioned air and the passenger compartment became extremely uncomfortable. I couldn't understand why we were not de-planing. Looking out the window at the terminal building I suddenly understood why…The sign on the terminal building read "MANAUS" ! I suddenly realized we were being held captive on the banks of the Amazon River, in the equatorial heat of Northern Brazil.

The wait was interminable…sleeping was impossible in the summer heat. Finally, three hours later, the sun began to rise and a new flight crew entered the cockpit. At last, the doors were closed and the engines started. Cool, dry air once again began to flow into the passenger compartment and I breathed a sigh of relief. As we took off and reached our cruising altitude, I moved back a few rows and stretched out on some vacant seats for a short nap.

I was awakened by the announcement that we were approaching Brasilia, the capital of Brazil, a totally artificial city built by "central planners" in the heart of the country. In the old days, I was told by a passenger, the military government could command that an airline make an unplanned stop in Brasilia to transport military officers. Today, however, we flew over the city uninterrupted. By this time Russ was getting very excited. Staring out at the landscape below, he declared, "We're actually in Brazil!", whereupon he proceeded to take out his English-to-Portuguese dictionary and examine the contents. I was less than amused...staying up all night after drinking Antarctica beer and trying to sleep in the heat and humidity had left me in no position to appreciate our whereabouts. Russ, however, was irrepressible. He had never been out of the country before and his excitement was grinding on my nerves.

Finally, at about 9:00 a.m., we found ourselves on final approach to Rio. I was much relieved. All I could think of was finding a place to sleep… Russ, however was becoming more and more excited. We landed in Rio and proceeded through customs. Immediately, our business visas were challenged and we were ushered into a private room, where authorities questioned the purpose of our trip. Finally, they were satisfied and we were allowed to depart. Not being conversant in Portuguese, I was somewhat concerned about identifying the CSN company representative who planned to meet us. Luckily, it turned out to not be a problem, and we sighted our driver with a large sign in English who planned to drive us in his limousine to Volta Redonda, a 90 kilometer trip. Russ tried unsuccessfully to communicate with the driver using his English to Portuguese dictionary, but finally gave up and just stared out the window.

Arriving in Volta Redonda, Portuguese for "bend in the river", we were escorted to the Sider Palace Hotel, a somewhat downscale residence used by visitors to CSN. We were told that the Bela Vista, the grand hotel overlooking the city, would soon be available and that we would only be staying at the Sider Palace for a short period of time. We were much relieved.

Now Russ was in his element. He was determined to communicate with the desk clerk at the hotel, so he searched in his dictionary for the phrase, "have a nice day". He found it and attempted the Portuguese pronunciation. The desk clerk just stared at him. Russ got more excited. He pushed the dictionary in the desk clerk's face and pointing to the phrase. The desk clerk looked blank. He was illiterate…

Russ was perplexed…he could not let this challenge go unanswered. Finally, as a last resort, he decided to pantomime his message. "You know," he said, smiling his best smile and waving his arms above his head, "HAPPY!". The desk clerk's eyes lit up…"Wow!" said Russ as we carried our bags up the stairs, "I actually communicated with him!" As we reached the top we heard someone running up the stairs behind us. Turning around, we saw the desk clerk approaching with a smile on his face. He stopped and handed Russ a large paper filled with marijuana. Russ was shocked…he gave the clerk five dollars and rushed into his room to flush the marijuana down the toilet…So much for the English-to-Portuguese dictionary…

I slept the sleep of the dead…I awoke the next morning to songs of birds outside the window. It was a beautiful day. I took a shower and headed up for breakfast. Arrayed before me was the greatest selection of tropical fruits that I had ever seen. Many of the fruits I could not recognize and some, as I was to find out later, were reported to be hallucinogenic. I settled on pineapple, which was delicious. As the days wore on in Brazil I would be less and less enchanted with the pineapple, which appeared, like clockwork, every morning. Apparently no one in Brazil had ever heard of eggs for breakfast.

But there were greater issues ahead of us…That morning we walked across the street to CSN headquarters and were introduced to our interpreter, who would stay with us for the duration, at least during our work day. The CSN office building was an impressive, newly built skyscraper, and we were whisked by elevator to the offices of a top executive. He greeted us in fluent English, and as was the custom, offered us a cup of very strong Brazilian coffee. We sat in his office suite and discussed our upcoming assignment, which was to upgrade the Honeywell 4010 computer system in the steel mill with modern peripherals, including new video, printers, and card readers.

This was not a trivial task. In modern computer systems, the I/O or input/output devices attached to the computer were on a "bus" structure, which meant that all signals to drive the devices were connected to every slot in the card file. In a modern system, the circuit boards driving these devices could just be "plugged in" to the slot after being properly addressed. The external cables that connected these devices to the card slots could then be connected and the system re-started.

With the 4010 computer system, however, this technology was not yet available, so each card slot that supported a new peripheral device had to be laboriously hand-wired for address, control, and data lines using 30 gauge (very small) wire and a wire-wrapping gun. A person could go blind staring, for hours and hours, at a computer backpanel with thousands of tiny wires connected to thousands of tiny pins. If even one wire were connected improperly, it could take hours to trouble-shoot the problem.

We thanked the director for the coffee whereupon he told us that he would be "glad to do anything to assist" in the upcoming project. We were then led by our interpreter back to the ground floor and out into the mill proper. Unlike the newer office building, as we were to quickly discover, the mill itself was almost 40 years old and showing it's age. We ascended the grimy stairs and entered the computer room, where we were introduced to the CSN staff. Luckily, several of them spoke English well and had been to Honeywell in Phoenix for training. We stared out the badly smudged plate glass windows to the mill floor where huge, fiery, blast furnaces dwarfed the smaller control rooms manned by operators, who, with the help of the computer system, ran the plant.

All went well and soon we were at lunch, which was very pleasant, in downtown Volta Redonda. Returning to the mill, I had one question which had been burning in my consciousness for several hours : "Where is the equipment from Phoenix that we are to install?" When we returned to the control room, no one seemed able to answer the question. Our interpreter offered to find someone to help us, so we spent the afternoon visiting mailrooms and maintenance offices to no effect. I was beginning to get a little "antsy", by this time, knowing that I had another job to complete before I left the country. Finally, it was late afternoon and all the offices were closed up, so we returned to our hotel. I was to discover years later that CSN, a government institution, only required their employees to work six hour shifts. In the 'nineties, some ten years later, the mill was privatized and workers were asked to work an eight hour day, causing huge riots and violence between workers and management according to The Internationalist, a Communist on-line newspaper.

But I was worried. I had to get this job finished in less than two weeks. Returning to the hotel, I found out that our reservations at the Bela Vista hotel had been confirmed, so we packed up and were driven by car up to the Big House, a stunning hotel overlooking the city of Volta Redonda and the steel mill. There, over dinner, I was to meet several Europeans, including a German, a Brit, and a Scot, who began to fill me in on some of the details of the steel mill. When I told them about my problem finding my equipment and my desire to complete the job in two week, they laughed uproariously and told me "no way". I pressed them for details and they explained that nothing, in Brazil, moved rapidly and according to plan. But it was not only a problem in Brazil. According to them, it was situation that existed in all countries in South America…And that reminded them of a joke…

As they related, a Venezuelan and a Brazilian, both English speakers, were discussing their respective native languages, which were Spanish and Portuguese. The Venezuelan said to the Brazilian, **"In Spanish, we say 'manana' for the word 'tomorrow'. What do you say in Portuguese?"**. The Brazilian replied, **"In Portuguese we say "amanan": However it**

does not convey the same sense of urgency!" Everyone had a good laugh, but I remained puzzled. Why were all these Europeans at the mill, most of them on long-term assignments? Slowly, over several Cachacas, the local Brazilian rum drink, the story began to unfold.

The year was 1943. The United States was involved in a war on the Atlantic and Pacific fronts and additional troops were desperately needed. The U.S. ambassador approached the government of Brazil to ask if they would supply troops for the conflict. The Brazilians were, to say the least, unmoved by our requests. Months went by without resolution. Suddenly, over a period of several weeks, 17 Brazilian ships were sunk by torpedoes just off the coast of Rio de Janeiro.

The Brazilians were outraged, but they were still wavering on troop commitment, so the U.S. ambassador proposed a deal: If Brazil were to send a battalion of 3000 troops to Italy to fight for the U.S., the U.S. would build a steel mill for Brazil and supply operating engineers. The Brazilians immediately accepted, and Henry Kaiser got the bid. But where to build the mill? After much debate, the site of a coffee plantation in Volta Redonda was selected. The plantation itself was uprooted and the construction began. The hotel in which we were sitting, the Bela Vista, had actually been the Manor House for the plantation, which explained its relatively luxurious accoutrements. Ever since the completion of the mill in 1945, my dinner partners told me, engineers from Europe and America had been supplying the technical assistance to keep the mill operational.

I was stunned. I thought about all of this new information as I tried to go to sleep in my new surroundings. Later, I was to discuss this information with an older Brazilian man working at the hotel and who spoke English fluently. "Yes, yes" he replied, "The story is true". And then he paused for dramatic effect. "And you know what we think?" "No," I replied. "Well," he hesitated, not knowing how I would take the information that he was about to reveal, "We think, to this day, that it was an American submarine that sunk our ships!" I was speechless...

I thanked him for the information and went to breakfast, running this story over in my mind. Was it true? I had no way to know…After breakfast, I walked outside into the parking lot to wait for our ride to the mill, which I could see down in the valley below us, shining in the distance. As I watched, the mill was suddenly obscured by a huge dust cloud…Seconds later, I heard a muffled "boom". The Brit looked down at the mill and then at me. Noticing the shocked expression on my face, he grinned. "Yep", he said, "That's where we're going!"

What was I getting into? When I questioned the Brit further, he explained that the mill collected scrap steel to melt in the furnaces. Because of the occasionally heavy rainfall, water would often seep down into the scrap collection bins and fill the bottoms. Operators would then lift the scrap bins by crane and move them to a position above the blast furnaces. When they were correctly aligned the entire bin would be dumped, water and all, into the gaping maw of the 3000 degree blast furnace. When the rainwater hit the molten steel, he told me, a steam explosion occurred, flinging molten steel the entire height and width of the building and shaking it to its foundation. Whenever this occurred, which was frequently, employees in the computer room would rush to the windows to see if any workers had been killed. Occasionally, they were.

That really caught my attention and I vowed to spend as little time on the mill floor has possible. But I had other problems to deal with that day; namely, to discover the whereabouts of the Honeywell computer parts that had been shipped in. Finally, working with our interpreter, I found that the parts had been stored in one of the many warehouses on site. I asked him to take us there, which he did. Opening the locked warehouse door we entered only to discover that Honeywell had shipped all the equipment using overseas shipping containers, which were giant-sized wooden crates. I stared at the twenty foot high pile of boxes on the warehouse floor. I couldn't believe it. I tried to communicate to a disinterested warehouse worker that we needed the contents of the boxes in the computer room. He didn't really seem to be responding to what I was saying, so I fell back on the traditional communication technique of speaking loudly and waving my arms to try to make him understand. Strangely, in Portuguese, "computer" is feminine: La Computadora whereas in Spanish, "computer" is masculine": El Computador. Either way, I did not feel reassured that we would see the equipment in the computer room any time soon and possibly not in our lifetime.

We returned to the Bela Vista for lunch and were joined by the Brit and Scot. While waiting in line to be seated, the Brit began an animated conversation with Russ. As the conversation developed, the Brit fell into the usual bilingual communication technique that was coming to be so natural to us, waving his arms and speaking in mono-syllables. The Scot had had enough…He turned to the Brit. **"Bloody Hell!"** he exclaimed, **"The man is an American. He speaks English, you know!"** We all had a good laugh…

We took the bus back to the mill. "This is turning into a nightmare", I thought to myself as I reviewed the drawings for the installation in the computer room and waited for the parts, which, of course, never showed up. I asked our interpreter if we could go and see the executive in the office building who said he would help us, but the interpreter shook his head in disapproval. It was not his job, he told me, to communicate with anyone at that level of management. He flatly refused to even take us over to the office building. I was frustrated. I needed a plan. That night I stared at the ceiling in my bedroom…Finally it came to me …

The next day we were scheduled to go to the main office building to receive our per diem expense allotments from the pay window. I would use that opportunity, after receiving our allotments, to kidnap the interpreter and drag him, if necessary, into the elevator, where we would take him up to the 9th floor and personally confront the executive.

My plan went off without a hitch. Our interpreter started to protest as we hustled him into the elevator but we listened to not a word of it. We got off on the 9ᵗʰ floor and entered the office of the executive, who was quite surprised to see us. As usual, he offered us a cup of Brazilian coffee, which we accepted, sitting on his overstuffed furniture and admiring the view from his windows. I explained the problem with procuring the Honeywell parts and he looked a little perplexed. "I don't know if I can help in this situation," he said, "I'm not too familiar with the operations of that department". "Uh-oh," I thought, "here we go again". But, he smiled, we smiled, we all finished our coffee, thanked him, and departed. I did not have high hopes that I succeeded. We rode down in the elevator in silence.

It was lunch time again, so we walked out into the sunlight and went back to visit one of the restaurants that we favored. We dallied long over lunch, hoping against hope that somehow, by some miraculous force of nature, that our parts might actually be arriving in the computer room. Just on the off chance that something might be happening, we stopped by the warehouse on the way back from lunch. There was the most amazing sight that I had ever seen… There were hundreds, so it seemed, of small men carrying these huge crates on their backs and heading, in a line, towards the computer room. I was overjoyed…It reminded me of the long string of Brazilian Army Ants that I had seen coming back from dinner one night.

I had underestimated the voice of authority. Coming from a democratic society, I did not realize the force that rank played in these countries. And then I recalled my visits to Spain when an employee of a Spanish nuclear plant told me, "If the Chief of the Plant tells you to do something, to die would not be enough!"

I was much relieved. My strategy had worked. Not only had the workers manually hauled all the boxes up to the computer room, but they had unloaded them and removed all of the packing material. There was nothing left to do but to remove the parts from their overseas, watertight bags, and prepare for the installation.

I was eager to start. The next morning I began my preparation for wire-wrapping the computer back panels according to the long wiring lists prepared for the project. I was not sure what part Russ was going to play in this effort, so I began to try to explain to him exactly what we were going to do and how we were going to do it. In the middle of the explanation, as I was opening cabinets and showing him the hardware, I glanced back at him and his eyes were totally closed.

I couldn't believe it. Whenever I tried to talk to Russ in any technical depth, he nodded off, still standing in an upright position. Later, I was to learn that this condition is known as "narcolepsy". There was no way that I could trust Russ to do this project. I reviewed in my mind some of the conversations we had had over the last few days. Mostly, Russ was interested in "chatting up" some of the girls on the site. They would both giggle and laugh and try to communicate with each other and Russ would pull out his English/Portuguese dictionary and point out words and the giggling would start all over again. As it turned out, Brazilian women, in the most part, were really "'hot" for American men and overlooked no opportunity to flirt with them. Russ was in Hog Heaven.

I finally had a solution. Through mutual agreement, I managed to move Russ out of the computer room and into the front offices, where he could chat with the girls to his heart's content. Every morning I would come into the computer room offices, exclaim "Todo Bem", meaning "good morning", or, more accurately, "everything is good" in Portuguese and then head into the back room to begin my day while Russ stayed "out front" and chatted up the female staff.

The project began, finally, to take shape. Instead of placing the video terminals and printers in their final location in the control rooms on the factory floor, I installed them in the computer room so I could test them once I had finished wiring the backpanel and inserting the driver cards. Once all of the devices tested out by running diagnostic programs on the computer, I planned to take the dangerous trek over the mill floor, in front of the blast furnaces, hauling the devices to the individual control rooms where they would be installed.

And so, the wire wrapping continued. In some cases, it was actually necessary to crawl inside the upright cabinets, bracing against the side panels, to perform the work. It was on one of these occasions that everything "hit the fan": There was a loud explosion and the cabinet shook. Luckily, I was braced into position and "rolled with the punch". I crawled out, asking the staff what had happened. As I had suspected, there had been a huge steam explosion in the blast furnace area and everyone was out looking to see what happened. Apparently, no one was injured, but the scars from the molten metal could be seen clearly on the sidewalls of the building, all the way up to the roof. I still had the job of crossing in front of those furnaces to install the new hardware.... It was a sobering thought...

But all was not work. Things were at last progressing smoothly and we decided to take the weekend off. I had gotten to know the German who was on long term assignment to manage construction in the mill and he invited me over to his room to discuss our weekend plans. He had a large, framed picture of his father, in uniform, on the desk. I asked about it and he told me that his father had been in the SS in World War II. It was important for him to explain to me that his father had not been in the SS faction running the death camps but in the SS that was the legitimate part of the German army. It was hard for me to appreciate that distinction, but I accepted his explanation.

The weather was beautiful on Saturday and the German, the Scot, Russ and I boarded the bus headed for the beach in Rio. On the way, the German managed to totally terrorize me by explaining that there was a history of these buses going off the roadway and plunging hundreds of feet down embankments. When we came to particularly deep ravines, he would point out the rusting heaps of trucks, car and buses that had met their end. I couldn't quite grasp the true horror of it at first, but he was right. The roads were narrow, the curves were tight and the cliffs were terrifyingly close to the roadway. I held my breath as the driver pushed the bus at maximum speed towards Rio.

Finally, to my great relief, the mountains gave way to coastal plains and we entered a section of smoother roadway that led us to the bus terminal in Rio. We caught a cab to the Copacabana Beach, walked across the Avenida Atlantica and through the deep sand to the water's edge. The German had been very specific. "Do not," he said, "bring your wallets or any valuables and make sure you stuff your money in your front pockets!". Although everyone else took his advice, Russ, the loose cannon, did not.

As we sat together on the beach, the German instructed Russ and I to go in the water first. The two of them would watch our possessions, which we were told to hide under the blanket. I took my carry-on case with camera and hid it as instructed but Russ, being Russ, left his watch and passport in plain view on top of the blanket.

And then we hit the water. It was warm and salty and the waves were high. We enjoyed the surf, but the bottom dropped off fairly steeply so we couldn't go out too far. Half and hour later, we returned to our blanket and began to dry ourselves off. "Hey!," exclaimed Russ, "Where is my watch?" Russ and I looked under and over the blanket, but with no success. The German turned around and asked one question; "Did you find your passport?". Russ replied that he had. "Then forget it," said the German. What did he mean? Where was the watch? The German was silent, but the Scot began to explain "It was the piranhas."

To fully understand the reference, it was necessary to go back a month in time to February, when General Electric had originally scheduled our trip. It was a mistake…The schedulers at GE suddenly realized that we would be coming down to Rio in the middle of Carnaval, a two-week celebration of Mardi Gras in which absolutely everything was shut down and the entire population of Brazil forgot their marriage vows and every other vow they had ever taken, and began dancing and cavorting in the streets in drunken splendor. Homicides during this period reached an unprecedented high. It was not a safe place for us to enter or to work at this time, so our plans came to a screeching halt and we were re-scheduled for March, which was still a summer month, south of the equator.

The end result of Carnaval, as I was later to understand, was a boom, nine months later, in the birth rate. Most of the new births were illegitimate, so the babies were shuffled off to government or charitable facilities to be raised. Often the institutions were overcrowded and totally inadequate, so the urchins escaped and formed youth gangs on the street, where they lived a life of crime, targeting the wealthy and the vulnerable.

The favorite hangout of the street urchins was Copacabana Beach, where they were known as "piranhas" after the famous flesh-eating fish that populated Brazilian waters. One of their favorite activities was playing "Pateca" a game that involved hitting a shuttlecock with the flat of the hand. The cock would be battted back and forth until one side or the other failed to return it, thus scoring a point for the opposing team.

These urchins would circulate around the beach, looking for "targets" such as Russ's watch. When one was discovered, the game would begin, and the cock would be hit closer and closer to the beach blanket until suddenly, it would land squarely on the blanket. Within what seemed like microseconds, and before the beach blanket owner could respond, a piranha would dive onto the blanket, grab the shuttlecock and, in our case, Russ's watch, and be gone.

Such was our fate…Russ was thunderstruck. "Well," I told him, "At least you still have your passport". Russ was not consoled and he complained bitterly for the next hour. Eventually, he calmed down. Russ, for all his faults, was really a good-natured person and he took things in stride, which was essential for traveling in a foreign country. Later we left the beach and contracted with a small boat owner for a tour of some of the offshore islands, which were beautiful. Finally, we returned to the bus station, grabbed a bite to eat, and boarded our bus for a long trip back to Volta Redonda. Luckily, it was dark, and I could not see the deep ravines or the crashed wrecks.

The next day we returned to the mill. We were entering the final phase of the project after an enormous amount of wire wrapping activity on my part, so I allowed Russ back in the computer room to observe the testing of the devices that had been added. I discovered several errors running the diagnostic programs which were caused, in some cases, by wires that I had mistakenly connected. Luckily, I was able to diagnose the problems rapidly and make the necessary repairs. Russ looked puzzled. "How did you make those errors?", he exclaimed. I could have killed him.

The moment of truth was now upon me: It was time to install the video terminals and printers in the control rooms, on the mill floor. Walking as rapidly as I could, and as far away from the blast furnaces as possible, I transported the devices to the control rooms and installed them. All the control rooms had large windows facing the blast furnaces, and I began to wonder how the operators protected themselves in the event of an explosion. When I asked one of them, I got into an animated discussion with hand waving and lots of gestures. Finally, I understood…I walked outside and looked up and discovered that, poised above the window glass was a huge bulldozer blade-shaped device that would lower down and cover the window in case of a blast furnace eruption. I shuddered…

I returned to the computer room. I had been busy working and I had failed to notice the progress that Russ had been making with the female side of the computer room staff. One woman in particular, had captured Russ's attention. They would giggle together over Russ's dictionary until they could work out a piecemeal conversation. The relationship was getting far more serious than Russ intended, however, and the woman was asking Russ to come over to her house for dinner and to meet her parents. Russ was panicking…her last communication using the Portuguese/English dictionary had been the phrase, interpreted into English as "I need it".

We were now finished with the project, several days ahead of schedule, but we still had our expense money, which lasted until the end of the month. I explained to Russ that we could either stay in Volta Redonda for the next several days, until our next assignment, or go down to Rio and stay at a hotel on the beach. Russ was in a major panic to get out of town, so he immediately voted for the beach option. He had not told his female acquaintance of his plans, hoping to make a clean getaway before his presence was missed. But as we stood on the steps of the office building with our bags, waiting for our transportation to Rio, who should come by but the object of his affection. I stayed well away from the two, imagining the conversation that they were trying to have. I don't think she needed the Portuguese/English dictionary to figure this one out. I laughed until my sides hurt.

São Simão

The CSN project in Volta Redonda was finished at last and we were on our way back to Rio…This time, however, we were traveling in style. Our rooms were at the aging but classy Ouro Verde hotel on the Copacabana beach. The translation of the name of the hotel was "Green Gold", which always puzzled me; in fact it still does. One of the niceties they provided, however, was a tunnel under the Avenida Atlantica, the main road paralleling the beach, so that hotel guests could access the ocean directly from the hotel. The Avenida Atlantica, it turned out, was much to be feared, although we did not realize that on our previous sojourn.

As I was slow to learn, life is Brazil was cheap, at least by our standards. Cars would speed along the Avenida as fast as possible and without regard to pedestrian traffic. I had been pulled back more than once by my Brazilian friends as, engaged in conversation, I was about to step out into a street, thinking in my foolish American way that the traffic would stop for me, as it would have back in Seattle. 'No, No!", they would cry, "These cars will not stop for you!". I was dumbfounded. I stood there, stunned, as they explained to me that it was not uncommon for a pedestrian to be run over in the street. When that happened, according to their story, the car would often stop and the driver would throw the body in the trunk, and then speed off to dispose of it. As I was later to discover, many of the deaths that occurred in Carnaval were for this very reason. I was in cultural shock…

I retreated to my room, vowing, never again to step out into the street unless it was absolutely clear of traffic. But I soon relaxed…The weather was nice and the hotel was air conditioned, so it was a pleasant to stay there without any particular responsibilities. I did some shopping for my wife in the local stores which were a block back from the beachfront; I ended up purchasing a beautiful amethyst ring. The stone was from the Minas Gerais or "General Mining" district of Brazil, which I would soon visit. The gold, unlike the usual 10 karat or 14 karat found in the States, was actually 18 karat, which was impressive.

But returning to the beachfront was a problem. When I tried to walk along the Avenida, I was accosted by pick pockets, prostitutes and poor women with babies asking for a handout. I dared not sit down in an open air café and enjoy a coffee without being harangued. I did feel sorry for them, however. As it turned out, there was no Social Security or welfare to speak of in Brazil and the poverty levels were extreme. I had admired the hand-set tile walkway that proceeded for miles along the beach until I ran into an elderly gentleman, probably in his eighties, stooped over in the heat, setting the tiles. To work or not to work was not an option for him. In this country, unless you were wealthy, you worked until you dropped.

I breathed a sigh of relief as I entered the peaceful surroundings of the hotel. Now I understood why, on every floor, there were permanent security people stationed, night and day. But there was one thing that I had not counted on. In the southern hemisphere, the seasons are reversed, which meant that March in Rio was equivalent to September on the East Coast of the United States. That meant one thing: a major pollen attack, most likely from ragweed or some Brazilian counterpart. I was suffering mightily… My sinuses were clogged day and night and I tried to stay in the air conditioned air in the hotel as much as possible.

Russ, on the other hand, was having a fine time. I did not keep track of his comings and goings, but I was relatively sure that whatever his activities were, they probably had something to do with meeting women. I was not disappointed when Russ confided in me that he had met some really exciting women who lived in an upscale district in the hills above Rio, where the temperature and humidity were not as high as on the beachfront. The women were celebrating a birthday and both Russ and I were invited, as I was to discover. I was feeling miserable with my allergies, so I opted out and decided to spend the day watching television.

Big mistake… The television set was aged and only marginally functional. I could not discover any English language programs so I picked the only thing available, which was 18 straight hours of Samba Dancing. That got really old in a hurry, so I read a book and dozed off. Finally Russ returned and tapped on my door. The party had been a huge success and they were very sorry that I could not attend. They did, however, cut me a piece of birthday cake and entrust Russ to bring it back to me. Russ told me the whole story. I looked at him but his face was expressionless. "Well?" I asked him. He looked away. "Russ," I said, "Where is the cake". Finally the whole story came out. Russ, the untrustworthy, had eaten the entire piece on the bus on his way back to town. That really made my day.

The next morning, we were scheduled to meet with General Electric. The company sent a car to pick us up and bring us to the main offices, which were in the downtown area. The subject of the discussion was our next assignment, at the hydroelectric dam site in São Simão, in the interior of Brazil, just south of the Amazonas, or Amazon area.

The situation at Sān Simão, pronounced "San Simone" was probably one of most bizarre business relationships that I had ever had encountered in my sixteen years with Honeywell. Even for Brazil, this was one was totally deranged. In weeks prior to the trip, I had gathered bits and pieces of information from project managers in Phoenix and from senior field people who had visited the site, but nothing really prepared me for what I was about to experience.

To begin with, it is important to understand the role that General Electric played in the early years of the age of process computing. Unlike business computers or personal computers, process computers controlled real, live processes in industrial settings, setting output valves, measuring pressures, temperatures, and flows and generally controlling the plant environment. The original process computer was the mainframe GEPAC 4040, to be followed by the GEPAC 4020 and 4010, and later, after the Honeywell purchase, by the mainframe 4400, 4500 and 45000. In the 'sixties, 'seventies and even into the 'eighties these mainframe machines represented the finest technical achievements of the day. GE was very proud of their accomplishments. The machines were state of the art and the first process computers to hit the market. GE sold them everywhere.

But strangely enough, this was the source of their undoing. In order to introduce computers into the industrial world, GE took every order "coming down the pike". Every machine was customized for its specific application, which meant untold hours of engineering at high cost. As I traveled the Honeywell world, I ran into these computers in refineries in Holland, in chemical plants in Poland, in hydroelectric facilities and steel mills in Brazil, in cement plants in Venezuela, in pulp mills in Canada and in nuclear reactors in Spain. Domestically, I found them running railroad "hump yards" in Pasco, Washington and Minneapolis, and. strangely enough, even doing data processing at the Internal Revenue Service centers in Covington, Kentucky, Fresno, California and Chamblis, Georgia.

Because of the high cost of individually engineering every application, the Process Computer Division of GE was running a low margin, which meant low profitability. To make matters worse, GE turned out to be its own worst enemy in that its salesmen, in order to sell a several hundred million dollar power plant application with turbines and generators, would reportedly "give away" the computer system at a minimal price in order to "make the sale". This drove profitability even lower for the Process Computer Division and GE finally decided to put them up on the auction block. Several suitors appeared, including Fairchild Semiconductor, but the deal was never consummated. Finally, Honeywell stepped up to the plate and purchased the G.E. Process Computer Division in late 1974. The GE service group, Installation and Service Engineering, or I&SE, was not purchased by Honeywell, so there was a major need to immediately create a new Honeywell field service organization, which was where I entered the picture.

But how could Honeywell make a profit from this business when GE failed? Honeywell's concept was two-fold. It planned to take orders and build computers for only three established markets: power generation, pulp and paper and chemical and refining. That way, it could build "off the shelf" software which could be used for each application, thereby cutting development costs dramatically. Furthermore, the purchase agreement forbade GE from further development of computing systems, thereby assuring that there would be no future competition from that source.

The deal was too good to pass up for Honeywell, so the agreement went down as planned. But General Electric continued to remain in the picture, as the years passed, making sure that its industrial customers and Honeywell maintained a good relationship. Unfortunately, in some cases, relationships became strained, so General Electric would often provide assistance in helping to resolve differences. São Simão, as it turned out, was one of their biggest headaches.

Oftentimes there were problems with software development or with unresolved issues that caused the customer to not fully accept the Honeywell computer systems, causing the "warranty period" to become more and more extended. In the case of São Simão, it was all of the above, so GE stepped in, as a third party, to assist Honeywell in sorting out these "final issues".

But "final issues" could not even begin to describe the situation at São Simão. The drama, as it unfolded, challenged even the most determined and most sophisticated of companies. It was a long story, stretching back several years, as I was to discover. To begin with, CEMIG had requested a fairly exotic system for their São Simão hydroelectric site, involving two, redundant, 4400 mainframe computers in the control room of the dam and two, redundant 4400 computers in the switchyard, connected to the dam site by microwave link. As was customary in those days, the entire system was "staged" in Phoenix, meaning that all four computers were connected in the final configuration while software engineers completed the programming that would make the system work as planned.

So far, so good. Development of the system went as scheduled until one fateful day when a call was received by the project engineer in Phoenix. The engineering manager for CEMIG, the Brazilian hydroelectric site at São Simão called to explain that they needed the system "immediately". The Honeywell project engineer was shocked. He explained that the software development was not yet complete. "It does not matter", the manager replied. Then he began to explain; CEMIG was under tremendous pressure from the Brazilian government to purchase only Brazilian computer systems. Unfortunately, the fledgling computer industry in Brazil was not nearly sophisticated enough to provide the kind of application that they required at São Simão, so they were resisting the government edict. However, the deadline was fast approaching in which no foreign computers systems could be purchased, so, as he explained, it was becoming a matter of "ship it now or not at all".

Honeywell complied and the system was shipped, unfinished, sometime in the late 'seventies as best as I could determine… And then the problems began. Software engineers were sent down, under the system warranty, to complete the installation. The software people would proceed until a hardware failure occurred, at which point they would pack up and go home. Honeywell would then send down a hardware engineer to fix the problem, after which the software engineers would return to finish their work. This cycle repeated itself again and again over a two to three year period, well beyond the normal 12 month warranty on the system, and caused great concern for Honeywell, who was paying for the service and CEMIG who had a system that was not yet finished. General Electric, the supplier of the turbines and generators, was caught in the middle. Russ and I, then, would be thrown "into the breach" as an absolutely last effort to restore the system to functionality. We were to fix existing hardware problems and then Russ would be on-site for a four to six month period to assure that the software people had enough backup to finish the system

I was concerned. One of the reasons I was selected, as I was to discover, was that the last Honeywell senior field engineer, Wayne, was "held hostage" by CEMIG and not permitted to leave the São Simão dam site for a month. He vowed never to return, so now it became my problem. I would have to train Russ so that he could effectively maintain the system before I would be allowed to leave. That gave me great pause…

The meeting at GE finally concluded and we returned to our hotel. The next morning GE sent a car to take us to the airport, where we were to catch our flight to Belo Horizonte, a distance of about 330 km. We boarded the VARIG flight and headed north into the Minas Gerais, the General Mining State of which Belo was the capital. It was a relatively smooth flight but a rough landing as we touched down at the local airport. Belo Horizonte or "beautiful horizon" was at an altitude of 3000 feet, so the temperature and humidity were much more pleasant than Rio. We were to stay at the International Hotel, which was a first class hotel, for a night before proceeding onwards. Our instructions were to take a cab to a specific street address at 9:00 a.m. the next morning, so we did as instructed, not knowing what to anticipate.

Finding the address proved more difficult than expected, but we finally located an old aircraft hanger in the "general aviation" section of the airport. We approached with bags and toolboxes in hand. Walking around to the front of the hangar we discovered a small, single engine, six passenger Brazilian aircraft fueling up on the tarmac. The doors of the aircraft were open and the pilots motioned us inside.

We entered the aircraft. The quarters were somewhat cramped, but I managed to get a seat as far forward as possible so I could watch what was going on in the cockpit. The doors were closed and we taxied out to the runway. Soon we were in the air and looking down at the landscape…and looking….and looking….and looking. No one spoke English so we had no idea where we were going or how long it was going to take. From the looks of it, it was going to be a long time…a long boring time especially with the radio blasting samba music. To relieve the boredom I unfastened my seat belt and leaned forwards to look into the cockpit. I was shocked…both pilots were reading the newspaper, paying not one bit of attention to other traffic in the area. These were the days before the Honeywell TCAS, or Traffic Collision Alerting System, so I knew that at least one of the two pilots should have been scanning the surrounding airspace for other aircraft.

I begin to wonder if any of us were going to survive this flight. After almost three hours in the air, there was still no end in site. Finally, the engine noise subsided and I became hopeful that we were descending to our final destination. No such luck. As we landed on the runway, I could see that we had reached Uberlandia. Unfortunately, it appeared that Uberlandia was only an interim destination. We loaded some packages and were back in the air again..

This was really getting old. It began to dawn on me that this aircraft was actually the CEMIG "company plane" and that it was essential for transporting supplies and people to the remote hydroelectric dam site at São Simão. Now I understood how our last field engineer was trapped on the site…The only way out was by company plane…I began to scheme…I knew for certain that we were scheduled, in two weeks time, for a meeting at the CEMIG office building in Belo Horizonte with General Electric and Honeywell, to discuss the status of the system. The CEMIG office building, I knew, was near the airport in Belo, so it would be a simple matter, after the meeting, for me to slip across the street to the airport, grab a flight to Rio and then home. At last, I had an escape plan! All I had to do was to sell Russ to GE, Honeywell and CEMIG as being competent enough to troubleshoot and repair their computer system…Hmmmmm, I thought to myself.

My thoughts were interrupted by the pilots' noisy conversation. We were finally approaching São Simão and preparing to land. I looked out the window…The terrain, south of the Amazon, was quite different than I had expected, generally treeless with tall grass growing on rolling hills. As we exited the aircraft we were met by CEMIG engineers from the dam site who, thankfully, spoke English quite well. We were greeted and introduced to our quarters at the "CEMIG Hotel", an older, one-story, motel-like edifice with smallish rooms but, thankfully, with individual room air conditioning. We settled in.

The next morning, I awoke to a strange, smoky odor. I showered and dressed and walked out onto the porch. Clouds of smoke were drifting by, but no one seemed the least bit concerned. I sniffed the air…Strange, I couldn't quite figure out what in the world was burning. I inhaled deeply a number of times trying to identify the odor, but nothing came to mind. Finally, I gave up and walked to breakfast. Our waiter spoke a bit of English, so I asked him about the fires. They were typical, he told me, when the weather was dry. No effort was made to extinguish the burning grasses, so they were just left to burn themselves out.

After breakfast, we boarded the bus for trip to the dam, passing through clouds of billowing smoke. Luckily it was only a two mile trip and as we reached the final rise before our descent, we could see the dam stretched out before us. It was an impressive site, over 400 feet high and two miles wide. The power plant section consisted of 6 turbines with generators capable of supplying a total of 1700 Megawatts. Adjacent to the control room was a switchyard which connected the dam to the power grid. We were much relieved to exit the bus and the smoke-filled air and enter the dam. I had begun to feel a little queasy after inhaling the smoke and was now beginning to have moments when I felt somewhat disconnected from reality, almost in a dream state, but still conscious of things around me. Being in this strange environment heightened my sense of disorientation..

We were ushered into the dam control room. I was struck immediately by the huge plate glass windows facing the downstream section of the dam. I stared out the windows... The discharge from the turbines roiled the water into a white foam.

Suddenly, I notice a tiny boat approaching the dam. "Isn't that dangerous?" I asked our host. "No," he said. As the boat approach the dam, I could see that it was actually a home-made canoe being paddled by a bronzed native. "The fishing is good downstream of the dam," our host told us. "The turbines stir up the water." I was not totally sure why that meant better fishing, but I let it go at that. I watched in silence as my host busied himself with other duties. As the minutes clicked by, I found myself being transported into a different realm: the juxtaposition of the ancient canoe and the modern, computer-controlled dam was like a worm hole through the space-time continuum: I was experiencing two ages of man simultaneously…I felt as if I were in a dream state…

I snapped back to reality…We were now being given a tour of the computer room, the control room with large consoles where operators attended to the daily operations, and the offices. We were then led down into the long galleries which ran the width of the power generation section of the dam, and which housed all of the control equipment. Every hundred feet or so there appeared a communication cabinet, whose function was to communicate with the generators and turbines below and to transmit data and receive commands from the computers by means of a data cable, which ran the length of the gallery. Many of the hardware problems, it turned out, were in this area.

We familiarized ourselves with as much as the system as possible before the bus came to pick us up for lunch. I would periodically find myself entering a "spacey", dreamlike mode, which would last for several minutes, disappearing and then reappearing a half-hour later. It was very disconcerting. That night, after work, I went out for a run, hoping to dispel my symptoms.

It was absolutely pitch dark as I ran along the road to the dam. The fires and smoke were still present and I could see the glowing embers of the burnt out grasses as I passed by. At a junction of the road, I passed the only gas station in town. I was shocked to see the fires creeping to within yards of the pumps. The station operators, I could make out in the dim firelight, were sitting out front of the station with their chairs propped against the wall, drinking beer. I couldn't believe it. I may have been spacey, but this situation was not of this world. I returned to the hotel, took a shower and turned in for the night.

The next morning the smoke had cleared somewhat and I no longer felt the "spaciness" of the previous day. I had an opportunity to discuss my experience with one of the other contractors, a veteran at São Simão. "You don't want to inhale that shit," he said, referring to the smoke, "There are all kinds of mind-bending stuff growing out there!" But that was not the worst of it. Running on the road to the dam, he told me, was even more dangerous. Large poisonous snakes liked nothing better than to crawl out on that warm asphalt at night. The picture of me stepping on a large, poisonous snake at night was totally terrifying ...I never went out for a run at night again.

Finally, I began to settle into the routine. Our work schedule was 12 hour days with weekends off, an arrangement which was fine with me. On foreign assignments, I preferred to work as many hours as possible to deal with problems, complete the project and go home. The extra pay was also an incentive. Living in the São Simão community was easy and comfortable. People were quite friendly and the CEMIG portion of the town was very pleasant, with company houses, a pool, sport courts and several bars and restaurants. We enjoyed playing the Brazilian game of Pateca and swimming in the pool. I asked the CEMIG employees if they swam in the lake behind the dam and they told me that "Yes, it is possible if you don't mind the piranhas". When they noticed the shocked look on my face they were quick to reassure me: "Don't worry", they said, "They are only small piranhas...They will only nibble at you a little bit". I started to laugh...I couldn't tell if they were serious or not but I didn't want to find out. I knew the local natives swam in the river, but I had no idea what the "loss rate" might be...I couldn't help but notice the strangeness of the "two tier" society in São Simão...The local natives served as maids for the CEMIG employees, living in small backyard houses and earning about $25 US a month...

Back at the dam, work was going well enough, but there was one thing that continued to bother me. The chief engineer at the dam had complained about the insulation on some of the wires in the control room, which had become soft and fallen off. This was certainly a new one for me... I had absolutely no idea what could be causing the problem, so I moved on to his next complaint, which was his non-functioning card punch. In those days, before magnetic media, computer data was stored on IBM punch cards. As crude as that seems by today's standards, punch cards were infinitely better than the paper tape used on some of the earlier Honeywell computers.

So I examined the failed card punch. By taking down the backup computer, I could run an offline diagnostic test to determine the failure of the device. First, I had to load the "minimum loader" card with the card reader. This card provided a program to the computer, which, when initiated, told the computer how and where to load the much larger card punch diagnostic program

I initialized the mini loader program, punched the card reader button, and the large deck of cards, which was the card punch diagnostic, began to load. When the load was finished, I initiated a machine language instruction to "branch" to the beginning of the diagnostic program.

Nothing happened. The chief engineer was right. The diagnostic program was running, but this card punch was "dead in the water". The blank punch cards waited in the hopper expectantly, but no card feed occurred.

What the heck was going on? I examined the mechanics of the punch and found that the rubber roller that fed the cards had turned into a soft mass of "goo", just like the insulation on the wires. Rooting in the parts cabinet, I found a replacement roller for the card punch, sealed in a plastic bag, and installed it, making sure the tension was set correctly. I initialized the card punch diagnostic program again and the Bull punch went through its paces, serially punching cards with varying data patterns. When it was finished, I put the cards in the card reader and ran the program to make sure they had punched correctly. Everything checked out.

But what would make rubber in the control room dissolve? I really thought about that one…Nothing that I had ever seen in the U.S. or anywhere else, for that matter, could explain the problem. Days passed… As I learned a lot more about the dam and about Brazil in general, the solution suddenly struck me. In Brazil, petrol was precious, so it was mixed 50/50 with ethanol, an alcohol that could easily be produced by fermentation of any of the many plants growing wild in the countryside. If you walked down any street in Brazil, you became conscious of a certain, sweet smell, which was the unburnt ethanol in the exhaust fumes of automobiles. Now I had it. That specific, sweet smell, somewhat diluted, was what I detected every morning when I entered the control room. I checked out the air handling system and found out that the intake was located in the parking garage in the lower levels of the dam itself. I couldn't believe it. The system was sucking in alcohol vapors from the parking garage and pushing them into the control room, causing all rubber products to dissolve. I was exultant…I brought all the evidence to the chief engineer, but he refused to believe me. I was stunned…The only conclusion I could come to was that the engineer really enjoyed the highly alcoholic air. "Only in Brazil", I thought to myself…

Months later I traded communications with Mel, a Honeyweller from Phoenix who had quit his job, divorced his wife, married a Brazilian girl and relocated to Brazil, where he was attempting to set up some sort of computer service organization. He and I had talked a lot about the problems at São Simão, a site which he had inherited after we had completed our final warranty efforts. We often discussed how difficult it was to get management's attention to resolve problems. In many ways, it reminded me of Volta Redonda. Mel eventually asked me to come down, on my own, to help him work through problems, but I declined.

As an ex-Honeywell engineer, Mel was smart enough to figure things out pretty well on his own, but he did have one experience even stranger than some of mine. Some months after our visit, Mel had contracted with CEMIG to spend one week per month on the dam site working on hardware problems. Every time he would return to the site, he would discover, after reading the system diagnostic print outs, that, on Saturdays, like clockwork, one specific communication cabinet would fail. Later, it would recover and run normally. This really began to get on his nerves. He could absolutely not come up with a fix. Replacing boards failed to solve the problem.

Finally, out of sheer desperation, Mel decided to stay on the site an extra day. On Saturday morning he entered the computer room and checked the printer logs. Everything was fine. The problem always began about 10:40 a.m., so he checked the system time again. Still nothing. Then, at 10:45 the printer began to print out error reports one after the other. It was the same communications cabinet that was failing.

Mel bolted out of the door and down the stairs to the galleries in the dam. Half way down the gallery he located the cabinet. He couldn't believe his eyes...In the room above the cabinet, the janitor was swabbing down the floor with soapy water and a mop. The floor was sloped so that all water ran towards a drain in the middle of the room, and then dropped precipitously some twenty feet to the top of the communications cabinet where it shorted out all of the electronics. Eventually, the cabinet would dry out and communication would re-sume…Until the next Saturday.

Mel immediately communicated his findings to the chief engineer. He was very pleased with himself…He had solved a long-running prob-lem. The chief engineer seemed disinterested. Mel packed up and went home. When he returned on his next trip, he was amazed to find that the problem had reappeared. No one had taken any action whatsoever. Finally, in desperation did the only thing he could think of…He tied an umbrella on top of the cabinet…So much for the science of com-puter analysis and repair…

We were now entering our second week on site. Things were going reasonably well and we had resolved a number of problems. We had also developed a habit of going to one of the local bars, after work, to kick back a couple of giant bottles of Antarctica, a Brazilian beer that we had grown to love, and discuss the day's activities. I had hoped to review enough troubleshooting issues with Russ to raise his level of awareness and competence to the point that he could take over the site.

A Brazilian man came over to us in the bar and introduced himself as Paco. I don't know if that was really his name or his nickname, but he seemed very friendly and interested in our activities, especially the problems that we had encountered. We were happy to discuss them, es-pecially since he insisted on buying the beer. It was a curious situation and I tried to find out more of Paco's identity. To the best that could determine, he was a CEMIG engineer, and possibly a manager from Belo Horizonte, the headquarters of the company.

As the days past, the routine continued. Paco would continue to buy us beer and we would continue to discuss the day's problems. He was sud-denly our best friend. I began to get suspicious. I had a feeling that he intended to use this information against us at our upcoming meeting in Belo, in order to get Honeywell to commit to further warranty sup-port. Finally, I had an idea. In the middle of one of our conversations,

I asked Paco a pointed question; "Has CEMIG gotten any value out of the computer system?" He fell into my trap, and began to explain, at great length, the enormous technical advantage the system had given them.

The Honeywell system was running a hydroelectric version of the SEER software package, an acronym for "Steam Electric Engineering Report". This software monitored turbines and generators and utilized the Sequence of Events digital hardware system, allowing the computer to "capture" an event, such as a turbine or generator "trip" and analyze the sequence of events which had preceded the failure down to a resolution of one millisecond. In layman's terms, this meant that the source of any automatic shutdown of a generator or turbine could be immediately determined. In the old, pre-computer days, the generator or turbine that "tripped" offline would have to be physically dismantled and examined to determine the cause of the failure, a process which would take weeks and would be extremely costly in terms of labor and lost production. As Paco was to relate, on more than one occasion, the cause of the trip at São Simão had been determined by the computer to be only at a "nuisance" level, so the generator in question had been restored to service in a half-hour, thus saving weeks of downtime.

I filed this information away for future reference. Finally, my sentence was up. After two weeks on site, Russ and I climbed aboard the company plane and headed for Belo Horizonte for our meeting with CEMIG, Honeywell, and GE. We arrived late in the afternoon, and were transported to the International Hotel, where the local GE representative and the Honeywell project manager from Phoenix would be waiting for us.

I took a quick shower and headed down the hall to knock on Russ's door. Russ was not ready to go upstairs to our dinner meeting so I waited…and waited…and waited. I did not want to be late, and since Russ was not forthcoming, I left without him. Walking to the end of the hall, I took the elevator up to the restaurant on the top floor. I greeted our hosts. As it turned out, this was probably the best thing I could have done. The first question I was asked by both Honeywell and GE was: "Is Russ ready to take over the site?"

I had prepared for this question. I was not going to be rushed, but also I was not going to misrepresent the situation. "Russ gets along well with everyone," I stated, which was absolutely true. "Also," I pointed out, "Russ is learning Portuguese and is communicating very well," which was also true. But could he take over the site? "Yes," I told them. The problems, by this time, were minimal, I told them, and if Russ had any further issues, he could always contact Honeywell in Phoenix, which was only a few time zones away, although several thousand miles distant.

They were satisfied. Before I could say more, Russ showed up and we all sat down to a well-prepared meal. The conversation remained social for the rest of the evening and we turned in early in anticipation of our meeting with CEMIG the next day. For years afterwards, Russ would accuse me of "selling him out" at this meeting. I laughed every time he mentioned it.

The next morning dawned bright and clear, as it always seemed to in Brazil, and Russ and I took a cab to the CEMIG offices. We ascended the stairway to the meeting room. As we entered the hallway, we sighted our old buddy, Paco, in one of the offices. We called his name and waved, but he totally ignored us. Russ was taken aback. We both knew what was going on.

The meeting went well. As expected, Paco presented our list of problems with the site. We countered, explaining the issues we had corrected. And then, the project manager from Honeywell took the floor. I had prepared him well. He documented the value that CEMIG had gotten value from the computer system, citing the generator trip recovery. Based upon the fact that our customer had gotten value from the system, the Honeywell project manager declared the warranty period at an end. He agreed to allow Russ to stay an additional several months and to supply an engineer to work out the remaining software issues. After that, he declared, no matter what the situation at the site, there would be no more warranty support from Honeywell.

I was satisfied. I slipped out of the meeting room before the final bell and headed across the street to the airport, where I had previously scheduled a flight to Rio. In Rio I changed my VARIG flight reservations so that I could go home directly with Pan Am, an American carrier. Unfortunately, the flight was totally packed and I began to wonder if taking Pan Am had been a bad choice. But bad as the Pan Am flight was, at least I didn't have to connect through Manaus and Caracas... Finally we landed in Miami. After taking a short hop to Atlanta, I was able to catch a non-stop Delta flight back to Seattle. What a relief...

Actually, as it turned out, Russ did well at São Simão. He was very good at asking for help, so he managed to contact the design engineer for the communication cabinets in Phoenix. When he explained the intermittent communication errors on the network, the engineer, after a few questions, diagnosed the problem as an un-terminated communication cable. Russ was a hero, at least for a while: That is, if anyone at São Simão actually cared. He did learn some Portuguese during his stay, at least enough to irritate everyone on site by picking Italy against Brazil in the 1982 World Soccer Cup. Russ was just being Russ.

Years went by...I would hear from Russ occasionally. One weekend I flew out to Iowa to help him diagnose a computer problem at a nuclear power plant. When the system was repaired and back up, we had a chance to exchange stories, and it was then that I was to hear the final chapter in Russ's career. The manager of the Denver Honeywell office had finally found a contract that he thought Russ could handle. It was the Colorado State Highway service agreement... Russ was given a Honeywell van with ladders on the top and dispatched to repair an electronic freeway sign that was not functioning. It was dead in the middle of winter...The temperature in Denver was a minus twenty degrees and the wind was blowing...hard.

Russ found the non-functioning sign, pulled the Honeywell van over to the side of the road and grabbed the ladder off the truck. He leaned it against the overhead sign and slowly began to ascend. The higher he went, the harder the wind blew, shaking the ladder with violent gusts. Finally, he reached the top. He opened the electronics box, took off his gloves and attached a hand-held device that allowed him to program the message on the sign manually. He was freezing…His fingers barely worked. He doubted that he could get the sign to work, but just for drill, he decided to give it a try.

As luck would have it, it was at this very moment that a reporter for the Denver Post was approaching the sign, on his way to work. As letters appeared, the reporter stopped, pulled off the road, and watched. This was no test message. Slowly, across the full width of the sign the text of the message developed: **YOU… CAN…TAKE…THIS…JOB… AND…SHOVE…** The characters had reached the end of the sign, but the reporter got the idea. He grabbed his camera, took a picture and headed to the office.

In the afternoon edition of the Denver Post, Russ made the headlines, with the message and the Honeywell truck clearly visible on the front page. Honeywell management was in a state of shock. Russ had done it again, this time in blazing letters…Convulsed with laughter, I could not think of anything to say. It wasn't much later that I found out that Russ had been laid off and was working in a computer store. His wife had also divorced him, which was no great surprise.

I heard no more of Russ until the 'nineties. Our older computer systems were dying out and I was in big trouble. I really wanted to get into the new Site Support Specialist Program which Honeywell had developed to train its service engineers in both hardware and software technology. Management was no help…No matter what I did I got "stone walled". They kept telling me that, in order to enter the training program, I would have to have a pre-existing customer commitment to purchase my services. Finally I worked out a strategy. I found out the name of the administrator in Phoenix who actually scheduled people for classes. He was easy to talk to, especially after I discovered that he planned to retire in two weeks. I told him what classes I needed, and he put me on the schedule, despite the fact that I had no customer contract. He was an easy mark. He didn't realize that I had no management approval. He probably wouldn't have cared anyway…His thoughts were on those tropical retirement beaches…

And so I managed to enter the TDC 3000 Site Support Specialist Program. It was only after several months of training in Phoenix that upper level management discovered the fraud. They exerted their best efforts to convince my branch manager to remove me from the program, but he resisted; after four months of training interspersed with work assignments, I graduated as a Site Support Specialist in February of 1992. The only problem was that, despite my best sales efforts, I couldn't interest any customers in the Seattle area in a Site Support Specialist Contract. Engineers at these companies would always announce, "We write our own control programs"…

What to do…I thought about it a lot as I flew down to Phoenix for a Site Support Specialist Meeting. And then I met Ray. Ray was an SSS on a contract at a steel mill in California. He wanted desperately to travel overseas and take a support position with the Honeywell Asia Pacific Group in Singapore. There was only one problem…he needed someone to replace him. As we talked, we slowly developed a strategy. I would fly down to the mill site in Pittsburg, California and work with him to learn the system. After six months or so of "overlap", he would go to Singapore and I would take over the contract at the steel mill.

That sounded like a plan. It certainly beat the alternative, which was to relocate to Green Bay Wisconsin or to take a six month assignment in Korea or Japan. There was only one problem. Ray and I had conceived this plan without consulting management. But it was better to beg forgiveness than to ask permission, so, after being outraged for a while, my manager finally conceded that it was a good idea. After six months of shuttling between Seattle and Pittsburg on a weekly basis, I finally relocated to California. I had narrowly escaped…My office in Seattle closed down a year later for lack of business…

For the next seven years I would run the USS-POSCO contract at the mill, writing control software, doing projects, and devising control strategies for the Kawasaki Multipurpose Continuous Annealing Line or KM-CAL, an effort for which I would receive Honeywell Technical Services Citation Awards in 1993 and 1995. It was a different world for me then and tremendously challenging. But there was one thing it had in common with my earlier career. The KM-CAL had gas burners, and hundreds of them…It was a symphony of combustion, and I was the conductor…One day I took one of the new engineers up on the side of the furnace to show her the combustion controls. The heat was intense and the noise was deafening. Her eyes got bigger…She stared at me…She tried to talk but her voice was drowned out by the noise. I moved closer so I could hear and bent down and removed my ear protectors…She shouted in my ear…"Is this dangerous?", she asked…I never laughed so hard in my life…

But my time was running out…More and more of my customers were making the decision to support their own computer systems. As I was contemplating my fate one day, out of the blue, I got a call. My manager, Roger, wanted to discuss our business opportunities... "I think we should hire a new person," he stated. I was really not impressed. All contractors had been terminated at USS POSCO because of the devastating effects of foreign steel competition, and business in general was down. I did not have enough work to sustain myself, and there was definitely not enough for a new person. Before I could comment, Roger continued: "I have a lead from a person in Denver who says he knows you". My heart skipped a beat. "His name is Russ and he says he worked with you." I laughed and laughed…and laughed. Roger could not understand my reaction…and then I told him about that highway sign in Denver…

CPSIA information can be obtained at www.ICGtesting.com
Printed in the USA
BVOW031146080812

297352BV00003B/142/P